10 Minute Guide to MS-DOS® 5

Jack Nimersheim

A Division of Macmillan Computer Publishing

11711 North College, Carmel, Indiana 46032 USA

For Thom Moon, The Moon Man, whose friendship extends all the way back to my college days.

And, as always, for Susan and Jason

© 1991 by SAMS

FIRST EDITION
FIRST PRINTING—1991

International Standard Book Number: 0-672-22807-6
Library of Congress Catalog Card Number: 91-60771

Publishing Manager: *Marie Butler-Knight*
Managing Editor: *Marj Hopper*
Manuscript Editors: *Ronda Henry and Charles Hutchinson*
Cover Design: *Dan Armstrong*
Production: *Brad Chinn, Martin Coleman, Johnna Van Hoose*
Indexer: *Jill D. Bomaster*
Technical Editor: *Herbert Feltner*

Printed in the United States of America

Trademarks

Contents

Introduction, vii

1   Starting Your System and the DOS Shell, 1

Cold and Warm Booting Your PC, 1
Responding to the Date and Time Prompts, 3
Starting the DOS Shell, 4
Quitting the DOS Shell, 5

2   Running DOS Shell from the Keyboard, 7

Keyboard Commands, 7
Changing Active Disk Drives, 9
Changing Areas in the DOS Shell, 10
Accessing Additional Program Groups, 10
Canceling a DOS Shell Operation, 11
Scrolling Through Display Areas, 12

*3   Displaying Pull-down Menus with the Keyboard
     and the Mouse, 14*

Displaying the DOS Shell Pull-down Menus, 14
Using Speed Keys, 15
Using a Mouse, 16

4   Graphics Display and Help, 18

Switching to a Graphic Display, 18
Getting General Help, 20
Context-sensitive Help, 22

5   Disk Basics, 24

Using Disks, 24
Different Types of Disks, 25
How Directories Help Organize Your Files, 27

6   Formatting a Disk, 29

The Basic Format Operation, 29
Assigning a Volume Label to a Disk, 31

7   Specifying Format Parameters, 35

Formatting a System Disk, 35
Specifying Different Disk Formats, 37
Using Multiple Format Parameters, 40

8   Displaying Disk Information , 41

Analyzing A Disk , 41
Displaying Information on Multiple Files , 44
Canceling a Multiple File Selection, 47

9   Creating Directories, 49

Creating a New Directory, 49
Expanding the Directory Tree, 51
Collapsing the Directory Tree, 53
The DOS Shell Family Tree, 53

10   Removing an Existing Directory, 57

Removing an Existing Directory, 57
Built-in Safeguards, 59

11   Working with Files and the File Listing, 62

The Importance of Files, 62
Different Types of Files, 62
MS-DOS File Naming Conventions, 64
Viewing the File Listing, 65
Accessing the File Listing, 68

12   Organizing the File Listing, 69

Rearranging File Listings , 69
Using DOS Wild Cards, 71

13   Copying and Renaming Files, 75

Copying Files, 75
Renaming a File, 78

14   *Moving Files, 81*

Relocating a File, 81

15   *Searching for Files with Similar Names, 85*

Using the Search Option, 85
Working With Search Results, 88

16   *Deleting and Undeleting Files, 92*

Deleting Files, 92
Recovering Deleted Files, 94

17   *Viewing and Changing the Contents of a File, 98*

Viewing a File, 98
Starting the MS-DOS 5 Editor, 100
Editing AUTOEXEC.BAT, 102
Saving an Edited File, 103
Exiting Editor, 103

18   *Creating Program Groups, 104*

Program Groups, 104
Creating a New Program Group, 105
Adding Items to a Program Group, 107
Selecting a Program Group Item, 109
Modifying a Program Group Item, 109

19   *Running Multiple Programs in the DOS
        Shell, 113*

What Is Task Swapping?, 113
Enabling the Task Swapper, 114
Adding a Program to the Task List, 115
Adding a Second Program to the Task List, 117
Removing Programs from the Task List, 118

20   *The Backup Fixed Disk
        Utility, 121*

Archiving Disk Files (The Backup Utility), 121
Starting the Backup Utility, 121
Backup Fixed Disk Dialog Box Syntax, 122
Backup Options, 123

21   Backing Up a Hard Disk, 125

Performing a Total Backup, 125
Formatting Disks During a Backup, 127
Backing Up Selected Subdirectories, 127
Backing Up Selected Files, 128
Backing Up Modified Files Only, 128

22   *Working from the DOS System Prompt, 130*

The System Prompt Alternative, 130
Temporarily Suspending the DOS Shell and Displaying
    the System Prompt, 131
Exiting the DOS Shell and Using Standard
    DOS Commands, 131
DOS Commands, 132
Entering DOS Commands, 133
MS-DOS Command Summary, 135
Summary, 140

Introduction

In the past, MS-DOS has been the operating system people loved to hate, for several good reasons:

- When you started an MS-DOS system, it greeted you with a cryptic C> system prompt, which gave no indication as to what to do next.

- Performing even a simple procedure in MS-DOS often required typing in long and complicated commands at this system prompt, commands that needed to be entered exactly as DOS expected them to be or it would display its infamous "Bad command or file name" message.

- If you knew nothing about how MS-DOS worked, MS-DOS itself provided no help.

Recently, Microsoft Corporation, the makers of MS-DOS, released MS-DOS 5, which eliminated many of the complaints that dogged previous versions of DOS.

Welcome to the *10 Minute Guide to MS-DOS 5*.

Because most people are pressed for time and need to be able to get up to speed using new software programs quickly, the *10 Minute Guide* leads readers through the most important features of the program in a simple, "no-fluff" format.

And, because most users don't have the luxury of sitting down uninterrupted for hours at a time to learn a new program, the *10 Minute Guide* teaches readers the operations they need in lessons that can be completed in 10 minutes or less. Not only does the 10-minute format offer information in bite-sized, easy-to-follow modules (making operations easy to learn and remember), it allows users to stop and start as often as they like because each lesson is a generally self-contained series of steps related to a particular task.

What Are the *10 Minute Guides*?

The *10 Minute Guide* series is a new approach to learning computer programs. Instead of trying to teach everything about a particular software product, the *10 Minute Guide* teaches you only about the most often-used features in a particular program. Organized in lesson format, each *10 Minute Guide* contains between 20 and 30 short lessons.

You'll find only simple English used to explain the procedures in this book. With straightforward procedures, easy-to-follow steps, and special artwork (called *icons*), the *10 Minute Guide* makes learning a new software program easy and fast.

The following icons help you find your way around the *10 Minute Guide to MS-DOS 5*:

Timesaver Tips offer shortcuts and hints for using the program effectively.

Plain English icons appear when new terms are defined.

Panic Button icons appear where new users often run into trouble.

Keyboard icons identify the keyboard commands that you can use to initiate DOS Shell procedures, if your PC system includes a mouse.

The System Prompt icon appears when there is a standard DOS command that corresponds to the DOS Shell procedure being described.

Additionally, a special lesson on entering standard DOS commands is included at the end of the book. You can use this final lesson either as a reference for more information or as a quick-guide to finding the commands you need in order to perform routine operations when working outside the DOS shell.

Specific conventions are used to help you find your way around MS-DOS as easily as possible:

What you type   The information you type is printed in bold type and in a second color.

Menu Names   The names of menus are displayed with the first letter capitalized.

Menu selections and commands   The options you select from the menus and system prompt commands are displayed in bold type. (The options appear in color only in numbered steps.)

Who Should Use the *10 Minute Guide to MS-DOS*?

The *10 Minute Guide to MS-DOS 5* is the answer for anyone who

- Needs to learn to use the MS-DOS 5 DOS Shell quickly.

- Doesn't have a lot of time to spend learning a new operating system.

- Is a new computer user and is intimidated by the prospect of using MS-DOS 5.

- Wants a clear, concise guide to the most important features of the MS-DOS 5 DOS Shell.

Whether you're a computer veteran switching over to MS-DOS 5 from a previous version of DOS or a budding DOS novice, the *10 Minute Guide to MS-DOS 5* will help you find and learn the most important aspect of using the DOS Shell, the interactive, graphics-based environment used to initiate many common MS-DOS 5 procedures. If your time is important to you and you need to make the most of it, you will find that the *10 Minute Guide to MS-DOS 5* helps you master this extremely popular—and powerful—version of DOS in a fraction of the time you might ordinarily spend learning a new operating system.

What Is in This Book?

10 Minute Guide to MS-DOS 5 is organized in a series of lessons, ranging from basic DOS Shell procedures to how commands can be entered at the MS-DOS system prompt to manage your total PC environment. Unless you're already familiar with certain aspects of MS-DOS, it's recommended that you start at the beginning of the book and progress through the lessons sequentially.

If MS-DOS 5 has not been installed on your computer, consult the inside cover for installation steps. The back cover of this book contains a list of the keyboard shortcut commands you can use to quickly initiate many of the DOS Shell procedures.

Note: The actual contents and dates of figure screen messages may vary from those shown in this book.

For Further Reference...

Look for these other SAMS books to add to your knowledge of personal computers in general and, specifically, MS-DOS 5:

- *The First Book of MS-DOS 5*, by Jack Nimersheim

- *The Best Book of MS-DOS, Second Edition*, by Alan Simpson

- *MS-DOS Bible*, by the Waite Group

Lesson 1
Starting Your System and the DOS Shell

In this lesson you'll learn how to start or restart your system, respond to instructions displayed during system startup, and move to the MS-DOS 5 system prompt or DOS Shell.

Cold and Warm Booting Your PC

You can start your system in one of two ways:

- Cold booting involves simply turning on your PC's power switch.

- Warm booting involves resetting a computer that's already running by pressing a Ctrl+Alt+Del key combination.

Pressing Key Combinations When instructed to press two or more keys at the same time (called a *key combination*), simultaneously press and release all keys listed. For example, key combination instructions are written as Ctrl+Alt+Del.

After booting, your PC will automatically load portions of MS-DOS 5 into memory. The system is now ready for you to use.

One note of caution: The warm boot method deletes any information currently *unsaved* in memory before reloading MS-DOS 5. *Always* make sure you save your most recent data before warm booting. Save using the appropriate steps for the application program you are working in.

If you are loading MS-DOS 5 from a floppy disk, follow these steps to start your system:

1. Place the MS-DOS 5 Startup disk in drive A and close the drive door.

2. Turn on your PC to cold boot or press Ctrl+Alt+Del to warm boot your system.

If you are loading MS-DOS 5 from a hard disk, follow these steps:

1. Remove any floppy disk currently in drive A.

2. Turn on your PC to cold boot or press Ctrl+Alt+Del to warm boot your system.

Depending on what steps you tell the Setup installation program to have MS-DOS 5 perform during startup, one of the following things will ultimately happen:

- MS-DOS 5 will complete all necessary steps without your intervention and then display the DOS system prompt.

- MS-DOS 5 will complete all necessary steps without your intervention and automatically run the DOS Shell.

- MS-DOS 5 will pause at some point during system startup and display two special prompts, asking you to enter the current date and time.

Prompt The term *prompt* refers to a question, set of instructions, list of options, or special symbol that appears on your PC display. For example, the default MS-DOS 5 system prompt is either a **C:\>** or **A:\>** symbol, depending on whether your PC includes a hard disk. What you enter in response to a prompt determines what your PC will do next.

Responding to the Date and Time Prompts

If MS-DOS requests the date and time, follow these steps:

1. At the Enter new date prompt, enter today's date in the format **MM-DD-YY** (month-day-year) and press Enter.

2. At the Enter new time prompt, enter the current time in the format **HH:MM:SS** (hour:minute:second) and press Enter. (Entering seconds is optional when responding to the MS-DOS TIME prompt.)

MS-DOS 5 uses a 24-hour military clock to record time, where hours following 12:00 noon are entered as **13** (1 p.m.), **14** (2 p.m.), **15** (3 p.m.), and so on. If you started your system at 4:30 p.m., for example, you would respond to the TIME prompt by entering **16:30**.

Accepting the Correct Date and Time Before asking you to enter a new date and time, DOS displays the date and time currently recorded in your system clock. If this information is correct, you can press Enter to accept them and move on.

Starting the DOS Shell

If MS-DOS 5 does not automatically run the DOS Shell during startup, wait until the system prompt appears and then do the following:

- Type **DOSSHELL** and press Enter.

After a few seconds, the opening DOS Shell screen is displayed (see Figure 1-1). Use this screen to initiate DOS Shell procedures, using the following display elements:

- The *menu bar* displays the DOS Shell pull-down menus.

- The *drive listing* selects the active disk drive.

- The *Directory Tree* displays and selects directories on the active drive.

- The *file listing* selects and works with files stored in the current directory.

- The *program group window* selects and runs programs and utilities you've organized with the DOS Shell.

- The *status line* shows the current time and displays information about how to use the DOS Shell.

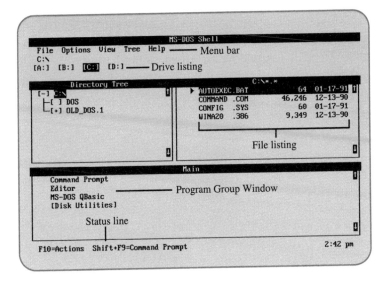

Figure 1-1. The opening DOS Shell screen.

Terminology Trauma Don't worry if you don't understand all the terms in the preceding list. Knowing how to use MS-DOS 5 and the DOS Shell requires learning both concepts and keystrokes. There are simply too many concepts to introduce and describe all at once. However, each of these items will be explained in more detail throughout this book.

Quitting the DOS Shell

If you want to quit the DOS Shell and return to the MS-DOS system prompt, follow these steps:

1. Press F10 (Actions) to activate the DOS Shell menu bar.

2. Press **F** to display the File pull-down menu.

3. Press **X** to select **E**xit.

5

In this lesson you've learned how to start your system and then how to run and exit the DOS Shell. In the next lesson you'll learn how to move around the DOS Shell display and select various DOS Shell options with the keyboard.

Running DOS Shell from the Keyboard

In this lesson you'll learn how to use the DOS Shell keyboard commands to move around in the DOS Shell.

Keyboard Commands

Working within the DOS Shell eliminates the need to memorize complicated commands to manage your PC environment. Instead, you can use a few simple keystrokes to initiate many DOS Shell procedures.

> **Keyboard vs. Mouse** Even if your system includes a mouse, you should be familiar with the keyboard procedures outlined in this section. Often, entering a keyboard command is quicker or more convenient than using the corresponding mouse technique. (Using a mouse with the DOS Shell is discussed in the next lesson.)

As a rule, you tell the DOS Shell to do something by either interacting directly with your display or selecting options from one of its pull-down menus. You can use the following keys to navigate the DOS Shell.

7

- *Arrow keys*—Move the cursor or highlight bar around the DOS Shell display.

- *Ctrl key*—In conjunction with other keys, selects DOS Shell options.

- *End key*—To move quickly to the end of a directory or file listing.

- *Enter key*—To tell the DOS Shell to begin a selected procedure.

- *Esc key*—To cancel a procedure or remove a pull-down menu from the DOS Shell display.

- *Home key*—To move quickly to the beginning of a directory or file listing.

- *PgUp key*—To scroll quickly up through long directory or file listings.

- *PgDn key*—To scroll quickly down through long directories or file listings.

- *Tab key*—To select different areas of the DOS Shell display.

- *PC function keys*—"Keyboard shortcuts" to bypass the DOS Shell pull-down menus and quickly initiate a procedure; different function keys have different purposes.

Pull-down Menus The term *pull-down menu* refers to a menu that remains "hidden" in a menu bar until you use the mouse or press a key combination to open, or "pull down," the menu. This type of menu gives you maximum space on-screen and still lets you get to the options you need.

Changing Active Disk Drives

When you start the DOS Shell, the drive listing window near the top of the screen is active with the current drive highlighted. You use this portion of the DOS Shell display to identify the drive containing the files you want to work with. The easiest way to change the active drive is to select that drive from the drive listing. For example, use the following steps to change the active drive to drive A:

1. Place Disk 1 from your MS-DOS 5 distribution diskettes in drive A.

2. Press the left-arrow key until [A:] is highlighted.

3. Press Enter.

This causes the contents of the various areas of the DOS Shell screen to change, reflecting the fact that you have made a new drive, drive A, active (see Figure 2-1).

```
                        MS-DOS Shell
    File  Options  View  Tree  Help
    A:\
   [A:]  [B:]  [C:]  [D:]
        Directory Tree                        A:\*.*
   [ ] A:\                          ▶ ANSI     .SY_      7,042  12-13-90
                                     AUTOEXEC.BAT          10  12-13-90
                                     CGA      .IN_     3,629  12-13-90
                                     CGA      .VI_    11,626  12-13-90
   Active drive                      COMMAND  .CO_    33,783  12-13-90
                                     COUNTRY  .SY_     3,913  12-13-90
                                     DEBUG    .EX_    16,816  12-13-90
                                     DISPLAY  .SY_    11,107  12-13-90
                            Main
    Command Prompt
    Editor
    MS-DOS QBasic
    [Disk Utilities]


    F10=Actions  Shift+F9=Command Prompt              8:03 pm
```

Figure 2-1. Selecting an active drive for your DOS Shell display.

9

 **Controlling Disks** Use the Ctrl key in combination with a drive letter to select a different active disk drive. For example, pressing Ctrl+C makes drive C the active drive.

Changing Areas in the DOS Shell

Use the Tab and Shift keys to change to a different window in the DOS Shell screen. The previous exercise, for example, was performed from the drive list at the top of the DOS Shell screen. To move to the program group window:

- Press Tab three times.

Or

- Press Shift+Tab once.

Pressing the Tab key cycles you forward through the DOS Shell screen areas. Pressing the Shift+Tab key combination moves you backward through the DOS Shell. Either of the steps above, for example, would make the Main program group window active, as indicated by the arrow pointing to the **Command Prompt** option (see Figure 2-2).

Accessing Additional Program Groups

Notice the brackets ([]) surrounding the **Disk Utilities** option. Brackets are used in the program group window to indicate an option that contains additional options. To select one of these, you must first access the second list of options. To display the Disk Utilities options, follow these steps:

10

```
                          MS-DOS Shell
 File  Options  View  Help
 A:\
[A:]  [B:]  [C:]  [D:]

      Directory Tree                    A:\*.*
 [ ] A:\                    ▶ ANSI    .SY_       7,042  12-13-90
                             AUTOEXEC.BAT         10    12-13-90
                             CGA     .IN_      3,629    12-13-90
                             CGA     .VI_     11,626    12-13-90
                             COMMAND .CO_     33,783    12-13-90
                             COUNTRY .SY_      3,913    12-13-90
                             DEBUG   .EX_     16,816    12-13-90
                             DISPLAY .SY_     11,107    12-13-90

                              Main
 → Command Prompt
   Editor
   MS-DOS QBasic
   [Disk Utilities]

   ─── Arrow indicates that window is active

 F10=Actions  Shift+F9=Command Prompt                    8:29 pm
```

Figure 2-2. Using the Tab key to move to a window in the DOS Shell screen.

1. Press the down-arrow key three times.

2. Press Enter.

The Main program group listings are replaced by a second list containing several Disk Utilities created for the DOS Shell during the installation of MS-DOS 5, as shown in Figure 2-3. You'll discover what these Disk Utilities do and how they are used in later lessons.

Canceling a DOS Shell Operation

The Esc key provides a quick way to cancel a DOS Shell operation or retrace your steps through the DOS Shell structure. For example, you're currently in the Disk Utilities program group. To move back to the Main program group, follow these steps:

11

```
                          MS-DOS Shell
  File  Options  View  Help
  A:\
  [A:]  [B:]  [C:]  [D:]
         Directory Tree                    A:\*.*
  [ ] A:\                         ▶ ANSI     .SY_     7,042  12-13-90
                                    AUTOEXEC.BAT        10  12-13-90
                                    CGA      .IN_    3,629  12-13-90
                                    CGA      .VI_   11,626  12-13-90
                                    COMMAND  .CO_   33,783  12-13-90
                                    COUNTRY  .SY_    3,913  12-13-90
                                    DEBUG    .EX_   16,816  12-13-90
                                    DISPLAY  .SY_   11,107  12-13-90
                          Disk Utilities
  →  [Main]
     Disk Copy
     Backup Fixed Disk
     Restore Fixed Disk
     Quick Format
     Format
     Undelete

  F10=Actions  Shift+F9=Command Prompt                    8:37 pm
```

Figure 2-3. The Disk Utilities options.

- Press Esc.

Or

- Use the arrow keys to highlight **Main**, and then press Enter.

This exits the Disk Utilities program group and returns you to the Main options.

Scrolling Through Display Areas

You use the PgUp, PgDn, and arrow keys to scroll through listings too large to fit in a single DOS Shell window. For example, the DOS directory created when you installed MS-DOS 5 contains approximately 80 files, more than will fit in the file listing window. To access and scroll through the file listing for the DOS directory on drive C, follow these steps:

1. Press Ctrl+C to make drive C the active drive.

2. Press Tab to move the highlight bar to the Directory Tree portion of the DOS Shell display.

3. Press the down-arrow key to make DOS the active directory.

4. Press Tab to move the highlight bar to the file listing portion of the DOS Shell display.

5. Press PgDn to display additional groups of files stored in the DOS directory.

For longer lists, you can use the Home and End keys to move quickly to the beginning or end of a Directory Tree or file listing. To jump to the end of the DOS file listing and then back to the beginning, follow these steps:

1. Press End.

2. Press Home.

In this lesson you've learned some of the basic keyboard commands used within the DOS Shell. In the next lesson you'll learn how to use both keyboard commands and the mouse to display the DOS Shell pull-down menus.

Lesson 3

Displaying Pull-down Menus with the Keyboard and the Mouse

In this lesson you'll learn how to display the DOS Shell pull-down menus. You'll also learn how to install and use a mouse with the DOS Shell.

Displaying the DOS Shell Pull-down Menus

You use pull-down menus to initiate many DOS Shell activities. Both the pull-down menus and the options they contain can be accessed using a single highlighted letter in the commands, sometimes in conjunction with other keys. To display the File menu, use the following steps:

1. Press F10 to activate the DOS Shell menu bar.

2. Press **F** to select the File menu.

Or

- Press Alt+F.

This displays the File menu (see Figure 3-1), which lists DOS Shell commands and procedures used to manage the files stored on your disks. Each of the File options contains a highlighted letter, which you can press to select that option once the File menu is displayed.

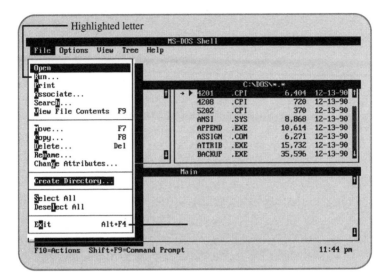

Figure 3-1. Using the File pull-down menu to initiate DOS Shell commands.

Using Speed Keys

Speed keys are function keys (F1, F2, etc.) or other special keys (Del, Esc, etc.) that you use, either alone or as part of a key combination, to perform such operations as deleting files, expanding directory listings, exiting the DOS Shell, and so on. When applicable, a speed key is listed on the pull-down menu next to the command it is used to select. For example, Figure 3-1 shows that you can use the Alt+F4 speed key combination to quickly exit the DOS Shell.

15

To use a speed key to exit the DOS Shell, follow these steps:

1. Press Esc to remove the File menu.

2. Press Alt+F4.

This returns you to the MS-DOS 5 system prompt.

Using a Mouse

You can use a mouse with the DOS Shell. However, if you want to use the mouse, you will need to load its device driver into memory before starting the DOS Shell. Use the procedures outlined in your mouse's documentation.

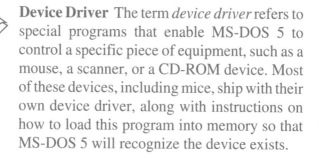

Device Driver The term *device driver* refers to special programs that enable MS-DOS 5 to control a specific piece of equipment, such as a mouse, a scanner, or a CD-ROM device. Most of these devices, including mice, ship with their own device driver, along with instructions on how to load this program into memory so that MS-DOS 5 will recognize the device exists.

Following is a review of a few mouse operations you need to know to understand mouse instructions in this book.

Point	Move the mouse pointer to an item on-screen.
Click	Press and release the mouse button once quickly.
Click on	Point to an item on-screen and click.

Double-click   Press and release the mouse button twice quickly.

Drag   Press the mouse button and hold it down while you move the mouse.

To try some of these mouse procedures, follow these steps:

1. Reload the DOS Shell, as outlined in Lesson 1.

2. Move the mouse so that the mouse pointer (a rectangular block) is positioned over the word **File** in the DOS Shell menu bar. In other words, *point* to File.

3. Click the left mouse button once. The File menu is displayed on-screen.

4. Point to **Options** in the menu bar.

5. Click the left mouse button once. The Options menu is displayed on-screen.

6. Move the mouse pointer off the displayed menu and click the mouse button. This closes the Options menu.

7. Double-click on **Disk Utilities** in the Main program group. This displays a listing of the Disk Utilities options.

In this lesson you've learned how to display the DOS Shell pull-down menus, using either keyboard commands or a mouse. In the next lesson you'll learn how to change the appearance of your DOS Shell screen and use the Help feature.

Graphics Display and Help

In this lesson you'll learn how to change the appearance of the DOS Shell screen. You'll also learn how to access the DOS Shell Help feature.

Switching to a Graphic Display

Regardless of the type of display you have, Setup initially configures the DOS Shell to run in text mode. When running in text mode, the DOS Shell uses letters, numbers, and symbols to simulate a graphic image. Notice, for example, the brackets ([ ]) around the disk drive letters in the DOS Shell drive list.

Switching your DOS Shell display to graphics mode allows you to take full advantage of your monitor's capabilities. Use the following steps to change your DOS Shell display to graphics mode:

1. Point to the word **Options** in the menu bar.

2. Click the left mouse button to display the Options pull-down menu.

3. Point to the Display option.

4. Click the left mouse button.

This causes DOS Shell to display a dialog box similar to the one shown in Figure 4-1.

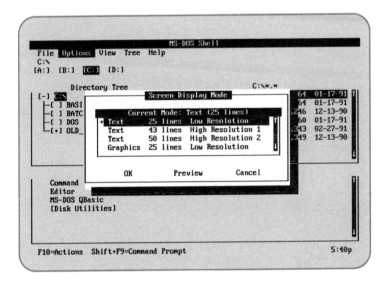

Figure 4-1. Using the Display option to choose how DOS Shell will be displayed on your system.

The specific options listed in the Screen Display Mode dialog box depend on what type of display monitor you have. (The dialog box shown in Figure 4-1 is for a VGA display.) To change to a different display, use the following steps:

1. Point to the graphics mode. (If your monitor supports more display types than will fit in a single window, clicking on the up and down arrows to the right of the Screen Display Mode dialog box will show additional options.)

2. Double-click the left mouse button.

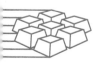

If your system does not include a mouse, use the following keyboard sequence to display the Screen Display Mode dialog box:

   1. Press Alt+O to display the Options menu.

   2. Press **D** to select **Display**.

   3. Use the arrow keys to highlight the Graphics display mode. (If your monitor supports more display types than will fit in a single window, you can use the PgUp and PgDn keys to scroll through additional display options.)

   4. Press Enter.

Dialog Box The term *dialog box* is used to refer to special windows that appear on-screen requesting additional information about a procedure. In the previous exercise, for example, the dialog box enabled you to choose the display mode for your system.

Getting General Help

Although you might feel comfortable working in the DOS Shell now, you may need help remembering exactly how to do something. If so, you can use one of the following methods to access the DOS Shell's Help menu:

- Point to the **Help** option in the menu bar and click the left mouse button.

Or

- Press Alt+H.

Press the first letter of an option or click on it with your mouse to choose the item for which you want information. For example, choosing **Keyboard** from the Help menu displays the list of keyboard-related topics shown in Figure 4-2. Selecting one of these topics either with the mouse or the keyboard displays additional information about it.

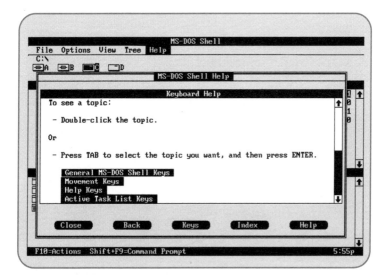

Figure 4-2. The Keyboard Help topic list.

When you're ready to return to the main DOS Shell screen, use the following steps:

- Point to Close and click the left mouse button.

Or

- Press Esc.

Context-sensitive Help

One advantage of the DOS Shell is that, to a degree, it's able to anticipate your actions, based on the display item you have selected. As a result, the DOS Shell Help feature will be *context-sensitive*. This means that it can provide information about the specific procedure you are trying to perform. Use the following steps to see an example of context-sensitive help at work:

1. Point to the **Disk Copy** option in the Main program group.

2. Click the left mouse button.

3. Press F1, the DOS Shell Help key.

This displays the help message shown in Figure 4-3, which contains specific information about using Disk Copy.

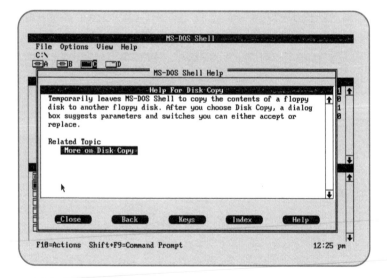

Figure 4-3. The context-sensitive Disk Copy help message.

If your system does not include a mouse, you can use the following keyboard sequence to display the Disk Copy help message:

1. Press Tab until the program group window is active.

2. Use the arrow keys to highlight **Disk Copy**.

3. Press F1.

When you're finished reading a context-sensitive help message, use the following steps to return to the main DOS Shell screen:

- Point to Close and click the left mouse button.

Or

- Press Esc.

In this lesson you've learned how to change your DOS Shell display from text to graphics mode. You've also learned how to access the DOS Shell's Help feature. In the next lesson you'll learn about the different types of disks available for personal computers running MS-DOS 5.

Lesson 5
Disk Basics

In this lesson you'll learn about the different types of disks available for personal computers running MS-DOS 5 and some of the purposes for which these disks can be used. You'll also learn how to use directories to organize files stored on your disks.

Using Disks

You use disks to store and organize the various program and data files you'll work with on a daily basis. Just think of a disk as a miniature filing cabinet.

File The term *file* refers to a collection of related instructions or information stored as a single entity on a disk. *Program files* contain the instructions that tell a PC how to accomplish something. For example, the program files for a word processing program include the instructions your PC requires to let you compose, edit, and organize a written document. You use *data files* to store the specific information a program requires to perform a particular task. You could store the actual text of a letter created with your word processor, for example, in a data file called LETTER.TXT.

Different Types of Disks

Most PC systems are designed to use two distinct types of disks:

- *Floppy Disks*—Floppy disks come in 5-1/4" and 3-1/2" sizes. To use a floppy disk, you must insert it into a disk drive of the same size.

- *Hard Disks*—Unlike floppy disks, hard disks are generally mounted inside a PC's system enclosure, making them a permanent fixture of your PC.

Floppy Disks

Floppy disks have the advantage of being transportable; you can take a floppy disk out of one PC and use it in another that has the same type of disk drive. The biggest disadvantages associated with floppy disks are their limited disk capacity and lack of speed.

MS-DOS PC systems can use several different sizes and kinds of floppy disks.

- 5-1/4" single-sided disks, which have a maximum storage capacity of 180K (very rare on today's PCs).

- 5-1/4" double-sided/double-density disks, which have a maximum storage capacity of 360K.

- 5-1/4" double-sided/high-density disks, which have a maximum storage capacity of 1.2M.

- 3-1/2" double-density disks, which have a maximum storage capacity of 720K.

- 3-1/2" high-density disks, which have a maximum storage capacity of 1.44M.

- 3-1/2" quad-density disks, which have a maximum storage capacity of 2.88M.

Different types of disk drives support these various disk formats. As a rule, disk drives are downwardly compatible, meaning that a higher density drive can also use disks formatted to a lower density, as long as that disk is the correct size. Therefore, you can use 5-1/4" 360K disks with a 5-1/4" 1.2M disk drive. Also, a 3-1/2" 1.44M high-density drive should have no problem handling 3-1/2" 720K disks. The converse, however, is not true. For example, you cannot use a 1.2M disk in a 360K double-density drive. (Of course, there's no way to insert a 3-1/2" disk in a 5-1/4" drive, or vice versa, so disk size is as critical as disk capacity.)

Hard Disks

Compared to floppy disks, hard disks are incredibly large—at least in terms of their disk capacity. You can use a 30M hard disk, for example, to store over *seventy-five* times the amount of data that will fit on some 5-1/4" floppy disks. Newer hard disks can hold hundreds of megabytes of data. Hard disks are also much faster than their floppy counterparts.

The biggest drawback associated with hard disks is that, being permanently mounted within your PC, sharing the data they contain with other users is not always easy. Hard disks, however, are quickly becoming the norm for PC systems.

Disk Capacity The term *disk capacity* is used to refer to how much information a disk can hold. Disk capacity is generally measured in *kilobytes* (K) and *megabytes* (M). Stated simply, a byte is how much space is required to store a single character—a letter, a number, and so on. A kilobyte equals 1024 (or approximately 1000) bytes, while the term megabyte is used to indicate *one million* bytes. A 30M hard disk, therefore, can hold up to approximately 30-million bytes, or individual characters.

How Directories Help Organize Your Files

Think about how difficult your life would be if your paper documents were thrown haphazardly into a file cabinet. Under such conditions, getting to even the simplest piece of information would be almost impossible. This situation is comparable to placing all your files onto a hard disk without considering how those files should be organized. Directories and subdirectories enable you to organize your disk files by grouping them into related categories.

One way to understand how directories work is to visualize the different directory levels, as illustrated in the following diagram.

Root Directory

   Level-1 Directory

      Level-2 subdirectory

      Level-2 subdirectory

         Level-3 subdirectory

   Level-1 Directory

      Level-2 subdirectory

In this lesson you've learned about the different types of disks available for personal computers running MS-DOS 5, as well as how you can use directories to organize your files (refer to Lessons 9 and 10 for more information on directories). In the next lesson you'll learn how to prepare disks for use with your PC.

Lesson 6
Formatting a Disk

In this lesson you'll learn how to use the DOS Shell to prepare disks for use with your PC.

The Basic Format Operation

Before you can use a new disk with your PC, it must be formatted. MS-DOS 5 performs several technical procedures when it formats a disk. The end result is a magnetic cross-reference system that DOS uses to keep track of the files a disk will contain. Formatting a disk is comparable to placing alphabetized manila folders in a drawer to simplify the process of storing and retrieving written documents.

The Fickle Format Syndrome Formatting a disk effectively eliminates all files it currently contains. For this reason, you should make certain that the disks you use in the following exercises contain no important files.

Use the **Format** option in the Disk Utilities program group to format a disk. For example, use the following steps to format a disk in drive A:

1. Place a blank disk in drive A. Close the drive door.

2. If necessary, click on **Disk Utilities** in the Main program group window to display the **Disk Utilities** options.

3. Double-click on the **Format** option in the Disk Utilities program group.

If your system does not include a mouse, you can use the following keyboard sequence to format a disk in drive A:

1. Press Tab until the program group window is active.

2. Highlight **Disk Utilities** and press Enter.

3. Highlight **Format** and press Enter.

This displays the Format dialog box, shown in Figure 6-1. You use this dialog box to instruct MS-DOS 5 on the current format operation.

You can use the Format dialog box to identify the drive containing the disk to format and the disk capacity you want it formatted to. Follow these steps to format a floppy disk in drive A to its capacity:

- Click on **OK**.

Or

- Press Enter.

MS-DOS 5 responds by displaying the following message, requesting that you insert a disk in the specified drive:

```
Insert new diskette for drive A:
and press ENTER when ready...
```

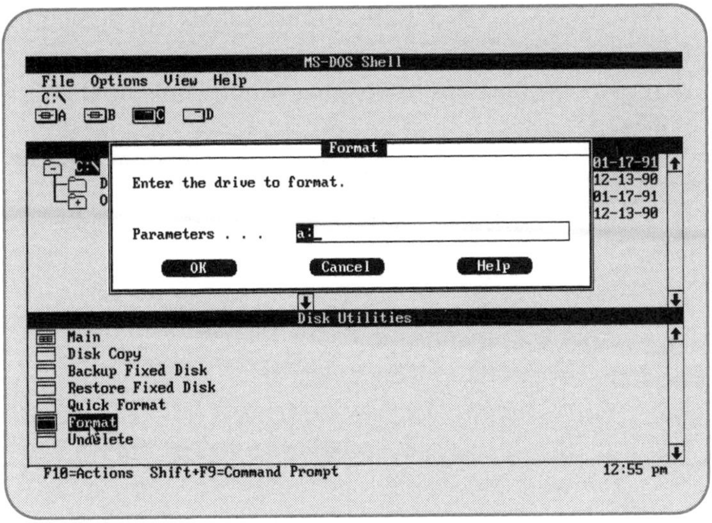

Figure 6-1. The Format dialog box.

After a few seconds, MS-DOS will display a status line, which it uses to report on the percentage of the disk formatted thus far. This status line is continually updated as the format proceeds, until the disk is 100% formatted.

Assigning a Volume Label to a Disk

As part of the format procedure, MS-DOS 5 asks whether you want to assign this disk an optional Volume label by displaying the prompt:

```
Volume label (11 characters, ENTER for
none)?
```

Note that MS-DOS limits volume labels to a maximum of 11 characters. When the Volume label prompt appears, use the following steps to assign a volume label to the disk in drive A:

1. Type **WORK DISK**.

2. Press Enter.

Pick a Logical Label One logical approach is to use Volume labels to provide a general description of what a disk contains. You can attach an identifying paper label to each disk, but what if that paper label comes off? Volume labels guard against this problem. You could, for example, assign each disk a Volume label that reflects its contents—89TAXES, 90TAXES, and so forth.

After accepting the specified volume label, MS-DOS 5 displays a message similar to the one in Figure 6-2. This message contains important information about the previous format operation, including:

- *total disk space*—The disk capacity, in bytes, to which this disk was formatted.

- *available on disk*—The amount of space actually available for data storage, following the format operation. This number will differ from the *total disk space* listed above if

  - You specified that this disk be formatted as a system disk.

Or

- MS-DOS 5 discovered bad sectors on the disk during formatting (see Panic Button message later in this lesson).

- *allocation unit information*—MS-DOS 5 stores information on disks in chunks called allocation units. While the values relating to allocation units displayed in the format message are extremely important to MS-DOS itself, you'll rarely need to concern yourself with them.

- *Volume Serial Number*—Each time you format a disk, DOS assigns that disk a serial number. You probably will never need to use this information either.

Finally, this message appears with the following prompt:

```
Format another (Y/N)?
```

Responding Yes to this prompt would allow you to format another disk without first returning to the DOS Shell. Follow these steps to return to the DOS Shell:

1. Type **N** and press Enter.

2. Follow the `Press any key to return to MS-DOS Shell` prompt.

What You See... The values shown in Figure 6-2 may differ from those that appear on your display, depending on what type of disk you formatted in drive A. The amounts shown here are for a 1.44M, 3-1/2" disk. Sometimes this listing may contain an additional value for *bad sectors*. When this happens, MS-DOS 5 has identified certain portions of the disk as being unreliable—not an uncommon occurrence, especially on hard disks. Unless the number of bytes listed as bad sectors is exceedingly high compared to total disk space, don't worry. DOS takes precautionary steps to guarantee that it will not use these questionable locations to store your important program and data files.

```
Insert new diskette for drive A:
and press ENTER when ready...

Checking existing disk format
Saving UNFORMAT information
Verifying 1.44M
Format complete

Volume label (11 characters, ENTER for none)? WORK DISK

  1457664 bytes total disk space
  1457664 bytes available on disk ——— Information on disk space

   512 bytes in each allocation unit
  2847 allocation units available on disk

Volume Serial Number is 1118-15E7

Format another (Y/N)?
```

Figure 6-2. MS-DOS 5 displays information about the format operation.

In this lesson you've learned how to use the Format utility to prepare a disk for file storage. In the next lesson you'll learn how to enter parameters into the Format dialog box to take full advantage of the Format procedure.

Specifying Format Parameters

In this lesson you'll learn how to prepare a disk using a format other than the default for drive A. In the process you'll also see how dialog boxes are used within the DOS Shell.

Formatting a System Disk

One useful way to format a disk is as a system disk—that is, a disk containing the files MS-DOS 5 requires to start your PC. The Setup program automatically copies these files onto your hard disk (or, alternatively, the Startup floppy disk) during installation of MS-DOS 5.

Specifying a disk capacity different from the default density for a given drive is also possible (see Lesson 6). This could be useful, for example, if you need to use a desktop PC to format a 3-1/2" disk that you will use on a laptop system with a smaller capacity. To format a disk in drive A as a system disk with this smaller capacity, follow these steps:

1. Click on **Disk Utilities** in the Main program group window to display the **Disk Utilities** options.

2. Double-click on the **Format** option in the Disk Utilities program group.

3. When the Format dialog box appears, type **A: /F:720 /S** and press Enter.

4. At this prompt, place a blank disk in drive A. Close the drive door.

MS-DOS 5 responds by displaying the following message, requesting that you insert a disk in the specified drive:

```
Insert new diskette for drive A:
and press ENTER when ready...
```

5. When prompted for a Volume label, type **SYSTEM DISK** and press Enter.

If your system does not include a mouse, you can use the following keyboard sequence to format a disk in drive A:

1. Press Tab until the program group window is active.

2. Highlight **Disk Utilities** and press Enter.

3. Highlight **Format** and press Enter.

4. When the Format dialog box appears, type **A: /F:720 /S** and press Enter.

5. When prompted to do so, place a blank disk in Drive A and press Enter.

6. When prompted for a Volume label, type **SYSTEM DISK** and press Enter.

After the formatting operation is completed, your screen will resemble Figure 7-1. Notice that the format status message now contains a line similar to the following:

```
118784 bytes used by system
```

This information was not displayed in the status message after you formatted a disk in the previous lesson. To understand why it appeared this time, you need to know a little bit about the various format options supported by MS-DOS 5.

```
Insert new diskette for drive A:
and press ENTER when ready...

Checking existing disk format
Saving UNFORMAT information
Verifying 720K
Format complete
System transferred

Volume label (11 characters, ENTER for none)? SYSTEM DISK

     730112 bytes total disk space
     118784 bytes used by system
     611328 bytes available on disk

     1024 bytes in each allocation unit
      597 allocation units available on disk

Volume Serial Number is 3C64-1CD7

Format another (Y/N)?
```

Figure 7-1. Using the /S parameter to copy the MS-DOS 5 system files to a disk during a format operation.

Specifying Different Disk Formats

As you learned in Lesson 5, MS-DOS PC systems can use different sizes and kinds of floppy disks. You specify what type of disk you're formatting and how you want it formatted by entering command parameters in the Format dialog box. If you plan to use a given disk to start your PC, then you must format that disk using the System parameter, (/S), as it was in the previous exercise. The disk will then include the special files MS-DOS 5 needs to load itself into memory.

Format command parameters supported by MS-DOS 5 are shown in Table 7-1.

Table 7-1. Format Command Parameters

Parameter	Function
/1	Formats a disk for use in a single-sided disk drive
/4	Formats a standard 360K double-sided disk in a 1.2M high-density disk drive
/8	Formats a disk to contain 8 sectors per track
/B	Formats the disk, but leaves enough space to allow that disk to accept the three system files for any version of DOS
/V	Enables you to specify a volume label for this disk, following actual formatting
/S	Automatically copies the DOS system files on a disk, following formatting
/T:	Specifies how many tracks should be created on this disk

Parameter	Function
/N:	Specifies how many sectors each track should have
/F:	Specifies the data storage capacity of the disk being formatted

Formatting a disk is a technical and potentially confusing operation. However, most formatting operations are fairly straightforward. As a rule, your formatting activities will be limited primarily to preparing either a system or non-system disk, designed to work with the disk drive on which it was initially formatted.

If you need to format a disk to a storage capacity other than that normally used by a given drive, you can enter the **/F:** parameter in the Format dialog box, as illustrated in the previous exercise. Valid /F: parameters are shown in Table 7-2.

Table 7-2. /F: Parameters

/F: Option	Resulting format
160	160K single-sided 5-1/4" disk
180	180K single-sided 5-1/4" disk
320	320K double-sided 5-1/4" disk
360	360K double-sided 5-1/4" disk
720	720K double-sided 3-1/2" disk
1.2	1.2M high-density 5-1/4" disk
1.44	1.44M high-density 3-1/2" disk
2.88	2.88M quad-density 3-1/2" disk

Using Multiple Format Parameters

As a rule, you can enter multiple command parameters into the Format dialog box. You did this in the previous exercise when you used both the **/F:** and **/S** to format a 720K system disk with a single format operation. Some exceptions to this general rule exist, however. For example, combining the **/1** and **/4** parameters in the same Format operation is impossible because each of these specifies a different disk layout and storage density.

In this lesson you've learned how to specify format parameters using the Format dialog box. In the next lesson you'll use the DOS Shell to request information that you can use to analyze the contents of your disks.

Lesson 8
Displaying Disk Information

In this lesson you'll learn how to display information about a disk, including its volume label, size, and the amount of free storage space it contains. You'll also learn the techniques for selecting multiple files for a DOS Shell activity.

Analyzing A Disk

You can use the **Show Information** option on the Options menu to analyze the contents of a disk and view information about the files it contains. Use the following steps to display disk information for drive C:

1. Press Ctrl+C to make drive C the active drive.

2. Click on the **Options** selection on the DOS Shell menu bar.

3. Click on the **Show Information** option in the Options pull-down menu.

This displays the Show Information message window shown in Figure 8-1.

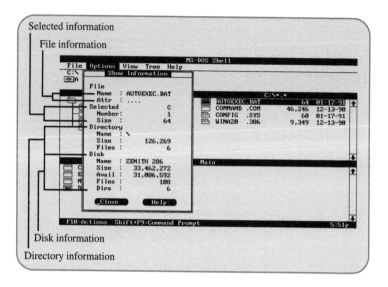

Figure 8-1. The Show Information message window.

You can use the following keyboard command sequence to display the Show Information message window:

1. Press Ctrl+C to make drive C the active drive.

2. Press Alt+O to display the Options pull-down menu.

3. Press S to select **Show Information**.

The Show Information message box provides information about the active disk, directory, and any currently selected files that the directory contains. For example, Figure 8-1 shows the following:

- *File Information*—The name of the highlighted file, AUTOEXEC.BAT, along with its current attributes. (File attributes are discussed in a later lesson.)

- *Selected Information*—The active drive (drive C), the number of files that have been selected on that drive (1), and the total size, in bytes, of any selected files (64 bytes).

- *Directory Information*—The active directory (the root directory, C:\), the total storage space required by the files in this directory (126,269), and the number of files it contains (6).

- *Disk Information*—The volume label assigned to the current disk (ZENITH 286), its total disk capacity (33,462,272 bytes), the amount of disk space available for additional storage (31,086,592), the total number of files on this disk (108), and the number of directories it contains (4).

When working outside of the DOS Shell, you can use a **CHKDSK** command to display much of the same information contained in the Show Information message window. Lesson 24 of this book contains more information about entering DOS commands directly from the system prompt.

Returning to the DOS Shell

To remove the Show Information message window and return to the DOS Shell, click on the Close button at the bottom of Show Information message window. This removes the Show Information message window and returns you to the main DOS Shell screen.

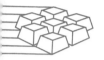 If your system does not include a mouse, pressing the Esc key removes the Show Information message window and returns you to the DOS Shell.

Displaying Information on Multiple Files

You can also use the Show Information message window to display storage information for multiple files in the current directory. This feature is useful, for example, if you need to send all the files relating to a given project to a co-worker or client. A quick check of the total file size would reveal how many disks this would require.

Marking Multiple Files

Before you can display information on multiple files, you must select, or mark, the files. For example, to mark the first, third, and fourth files in the current directory listing, follow these steps:

1. Click on the file name at the top of your current directory listing.

2. Point to the third file name listed in the current directory.

3. Hold down the Ctrl key while you click the left mouse button.

4. Point to the fourth file name listed in the current directory.

5. Hold down the Ctrl key while you click the left mouse button.

6. Release the Ctrl key.

This marks the three specified files, as shown in Figure 8-2. Selecting files in this manner makes them available for additional processing, such as analyzing their total storage requirements using the **Show Information** option, copying or moving them to a new location, deleting them, and so forth.

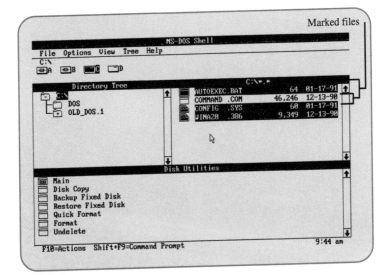

Figure 8-2. Marking multiple files.

To select multiple files from the keyboard:

1. Press Tab to highlight the file listing.

2. Press Shift+F8 to switch file selection to Add mode.

45

3. Use the arrow keys, if necessary, to position the highlight bar on the first file name.

4. Press Spacebar to select this file.

5. Press the down-arrow key twice to position the highlight bar on the third file name.

6. Press Spacebar to select this file.

7. Press the down-arrow key to position the highlight bar on the fourth file name.

8. Press Spacebar to select this file.

9. Press Shift+F8 to turn off Add mode.

Viewing Storage Requirements for Multiple Files

You can now call up the Show Information message window to determine the storage requirements of the selected files.

1. Click on the **Options** selection on the DOS Shell menu bar.

2. Click on the **Show Information** option in the Options pull-down menu.

This displays the Show Information message window as shown in Figure 8-3. Notice that, in this figure, the values listed in the section marked `Selected` now reflect the total storage requirements of the three marked files.

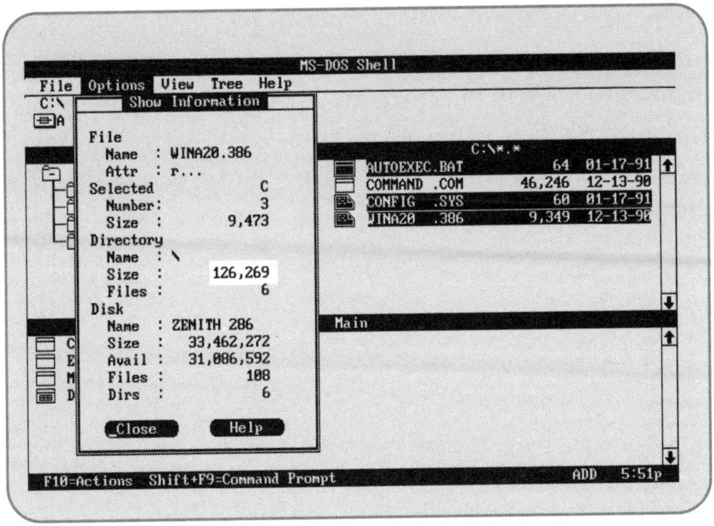

Figure 8-3. Viewing the storage requirements of multiple files.

After reviewing this information, click on the OK button to remove the Show Information message window and return to the main DOS Shell screen.

Canceling a Multiple File Selection

At this point, the three files specified in the previous exercise are still marked as being selected. To cancel multiple file selection and return to a single file, follow these steps:

- Click on any file name.

Or

- Press the Spacebar.

47

In this lesson you've learned how to access the Show Information message window, which can be used to display information about the currently active disk, its directories, and selected files. In the next lesson you'll begin examining how to use directories to organize your disks and the files they contain.

Lesson 9
Creating
Directories

In this lesson you'll learn how to use the DOS Shell to create disk directories, which organize your disks and the files they contain.

Creating a New Directory

In Lesson 5 you learned how to use directories to help organize your disk files. The Setup program already started this process when it installed MS-DOS 5 on your system. At that time, Setup created a special subdirectory called DOS into which it copied the various MS-DOS 5 files.

You'll eventually expand this initial directory structure by adding directories and subdirectories to your disks. An extremely useful directory is one designed to hold a special type of file called a batch file, which is used to automate DOS operations.

Follow these steps to create a directory called BATCH running off the root directory of drive C:

1. Make drive C the active disk drive.

2. Select the root directory (C:\) in the Directory Tree portion of your DOS Shell screen.

3. Choose the File option of the DOS Shell menu bar.

4. Choose Create Directory from the File pull-down menu.

This displays the Create Directory dialog box shown in Figure 9-1. You use this dialog box to specify the name you want assigned to the new directory. To create a new directory called BATCH:

1. Type BATCH.

2. Press Enter.

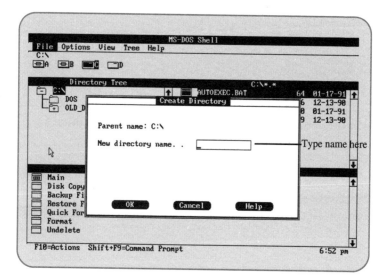

Figure 9-1. The Create Directory dialog box.

MS-DOS 5 creates the new directory and returns you to the main DOS Shell screen. As Figure 9-2 illustrates, a new directory, BATCH, has been added to your Directory Tree. Because you were in the root directory when you initiated the Create Directory procedure, this new directory is automatically made a first-level subdirectory running off the **C:** directory.

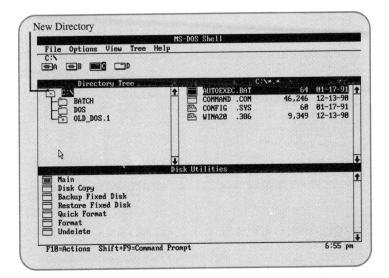

Figure 9-2. The new BATCH directory as a first-level subdirectory running off the C:\ root directory.

When working directly from the system prompt, you can use the MS-DOS 5 **MD** (Make Directory) command to create new subdirectories.

Expanding the Directory Tree

A plus sign (+) in a file folder icon next to the directory name indicates that there are additional subdirectories in that directory that are not currently shown. This is illustrated on the OLD_DOS.1 directory in Figure 9-2. To view the subdirectories in a directory:

51

• Click on the plus sign.

This "expands" the current Directory Tree listing to include any subdirectory running off the selected directory, as illustrated by the NETS directory running off OLD_DOS.1 in Figure 9-3.

```
                          MS-DOS Shell
  File  Options  View  Tree  Help
  C:\OLD_DOS.1
  ⊟A  ⊟B  ■C  ⊐D

        Directory Tree                C:\OLD_DOS.1\*.*
  ⊟ C:\                         ↑   ⊞ DISK0   .NUL        0  01-17-91 ↑
    ┌─┐ BATCH                       ⊞ DISK1   .NUL        0  01-17-91
    ├─┐ DOS                         ⊞ DISK10  .NUL        0  01-17-91
    └─┐ OLD_DOS.1                   ⊞ DISK11  .NUL        0  01-17-91
      └─┐ NETS                      ⊞ DISK12  .NUL        0  01-17-91
         │                          ⊞ DISK13  .NUL        0  01-17-91
      Subdirectory                  ⊞ DISK14  .NUL        0  01-17-91
                                    ⊞ DISK2   .NUL        0  01-17-91
                              ↓     ⊞ DISK3   .NUL        0  01-17-91 ↓
                             Disk Utilities
  ▦ Main                                                              ↑
  ▤ Disk Copy
  ▤ Backup Fixed Disk
  ▤ Restore Fixed Disk
  ▤ Quick Format
  ▤ Format
  ▤ Undelete

  F10=Actions  Shift+F9=Command Prompt                    7:22 pm
```

Figure 9-3. Clicking on a file folder with a plus sign to view subdirectories of the corresponding directory.

To expand a directory tree using the keyboard:

1. Highlight the directory for which you want to view a Directory Tree.

2. Press Alt+T to access the Tree pull-down menu.

3. Press **X** to select **Expand One Level**.

Collapsing the Directory Tree

A minus sign (–) in a directory's file folder icon indicates that the subdirectories currently displayed under that directory can be "collapsed" back into the Directory Tree. (Again, look at the OLD_DOS.1 directory file folder in Figure 9-3.) To remove from view the subdirectories running off a directory:

- Click on the minus sign in the file folder to the left of the directory listing.

  To collapse a directory tree using the keyboard:

  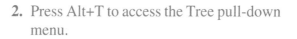

  1. Highlight the directory for which you want to collapse a Directory Tree.

  2. Press Alt+T to access the Tree pull-down menu.

  3. Press C to select **Collapse Branch**.

This "collapses" the current Directory Tree listing to remove the NETS subdirectory from the DOS Shell screen.

The DOS Shell Family Tree

The DOS Shell uses specific terminology to describe the various elements of your directory structure. Use the following steps to prepare for the next exercise:

1. Click on the DOS directory (DOS) in the Directory Tree portion of your DOS Shell screen.

2. Choose the File option on the DOS Shell menu bar.

3. Choose **Create Directory** from the File pull-down menu.

4. When the Create Directory dialog box appears, type **BASIC** and then press Enter.

To create a BASIC subdirectory using the keyboard:

1. Highlight the DOS directory listing (**DOS**).

2. Press Alt+F to access the File pull-down menu.

3. Press **E** to select **Create Directory**.

4. When the Create Directory dialog box appears, type **BASIC** and then press Enter.

Now that you have created a third-level directory, you can use the following step to analyze the terminology used by the DOS Shell to describe a disk's directory structure:

• Click on the **Tree** option on the DOS Shell menu bar.

To display the Tree menu from the keyboard:

• Press Alt+T to access the Tree pull-down menu.

This displays the Tree pull-down menu shown in Figure 9-4. The C:\DOS directory is itself both a "child" and "parent" directory—that means, it is a subdirectory of the C:\ root directory and has the BASIC subdirectory running off it. Therefore, this menu lists all the available Tree operations. These options include:

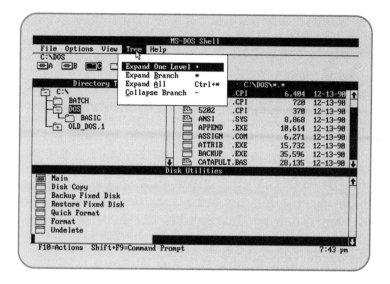

Figure 9-4. The Tree options.

- *Expand One Level*—In MS-DOS 5, a level is a single layer of subdirectories, directly below the currently active directory. Selecting this option is similar to choosing the plus key (+); it adds the next layer of subdirectories to the DOS Shell display.

- *Expand Branch*—A branch is the current directory plus *all* directories and subdirectories below it. Selecting this option (or pressing the asterisk key) causes MS-DOS 5 to display all directories and subdirectories running off the active directory, regardless of how far down its directory structure extends.

- *Expand All*—Selecting this option, or pressing and holding the **Ctrl** key while you press the asterisk key (*), causes all levels of directories and subdirectories on the current drive to be included in the DOS Shell display.

- *Collapse Branch*—This option, or its corresponding minus key (–) keystroke, removes all directories and subdirectories running off the active directory from the DOS Shell display.

After studying these options, press Esc to remove the Tree menu.

In this lesson you've learned how to create disk directories in the DOS Shell. You also learned how to navigate and manage the DOS Directory Tree, using the mouse or the keyboard commands. In the next lesson you'll learn how to remove outdated directories from your disks and, by extension, the DOS Shell screen.

Lesson 10
Removing an Existing Directory

In this lesson you'll learn a very simple but important DOS Shell procedure: the steps required to remove unwanted directories from your disks.

Removing an Existing Directory

Nothing lasts forever. Not even the usefulness of a DOS directory. In fact, one of the major attractions of setting up and maintaining an organized DOS directory structure is its dynamic nature. You can modify your PC environment on demand—adding a new directory when a situation calls for one, and removing it when you no longer need it.

In the preceding lesson you created a BASIC subdirectory running off the DOS directory. You did this so that you could examine all the options listed on the Tree pull-down menu. Having done so, you no longer need this directory. Use the following steps to remove the BASIC subdirectory:

1. Click on the **BASIC** subdirectory running off C:\DOS in the Directory Tree portion of the DOS Shell screen.

2. Click on **File** in the main menu bar.

3. Click on the **Delete** option.

To remove the BASIC directory using the keyboard:

1. Highlight the **BASIC** subdirectory.

2. Press Alt+F to access the File pull-down menu.

3. Press **D** to select **Delete**.

This displays the Delete Directory Confirmation dialog box shown in Figure 10-1. As this dialog box demonstrates, the DOS Shell generally prompts you to verify potentially destructive operations—removing directories, erasing files, formatting disks, and so on.

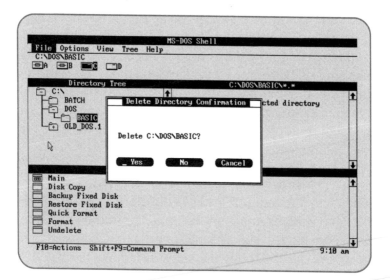

Figure 10-1. The Delete Directory Confirmation dialog box asking you to verify that you want a directory deleted.

Use the following steps to have MS-DOS 5 delete this directory:

- Double-click on **Yes.**

Or

- Press Enter to accept **Yes,** the default response.

You are now back at the main DOS Shell screen. Notice, however, that the BASIC subdirectory is no longer visible. Furthermore, there is no longer a plus or minus sign next to the DOS directory name in the Directory Tree portion of the DOS Shell screen. This indicates that the BASIC directory has been completely removed from your disk, rather than just hidden from view as was the case in the previous lesson.

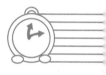

Pushing The Button The Delete command is one of the DOS Shell procedures for which a keyboard shortcut exists. After selecting the directory you want to delete, pressing the Del key allows you to bypass the File pull-down menu and initiate a delete directory operation using a single keystroke.

Built-in Safeguards

MS-DOS 5 and the DOS Shell go to great lengths to protect you from accidentally performing potentially destructive activities. Even when a directory is empty, as was the case in the previous exercise, the DOS Shell will not remove that directory without first displaying the Delete Directory Confirmation dialog box shown in Figure 10-1. Use the following steps to examine another safeguard built into the DOS Shell:

1. Click on **File** in the main menu bar.

2. Click on the **Delete** option.

Or

• Press the Del key.

Because DOS was the active directory, you may have expected this to erase all your MS-DOS 5 files and remove that directory from the DOS Shell display. It did not because a directory must be completely empty—that is, contain no files—before the DOS Shell will allow you to remove it. See the message box shown Figure 10-2.

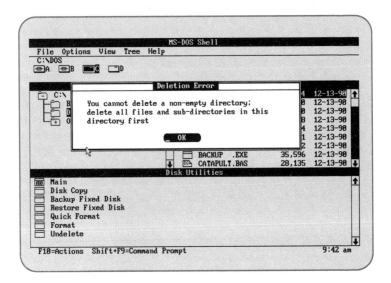

Figure 10-2. An error message box.

When you request that a directory be removed, MS-DOS 5 assumes that you no longer need the files previously stored in that directory. The DOS Shell supports this assumption by insisting that a directory be completely empty before deleting it. The error message shown in Figure 10-2 appeared because MS-DOS 5 scanned your DOS subdirectory and found that it still contained files. You need to erase these files before MS-DOS 5 will allow you to delete the DOS directory.

Use the following steps to remove the Deletion Error message from your DOS Shell screen:

• Double-click on Close.

Or

• Press Enter.

When working directly from the system prompt, you can use the MS-DOS 5 **RD** (Remove Directory) command to delete unwanted directories and subdirectories from your disks.

In this lesson you've learned how to remove directories from your disks and, by extension, from the DOS Shell Directory Tree display. You've also seen how MS-DOS 5 provides some protection against accidentally performing certain operations. In the next lesson you'll begin learning the DOS Shell procedures used to manage the most critical component of your PC environment, disk files.

Working with Files and the File Listing

In this lesson you'll begin learning the DOS Shell procedures used to manage the individual files stored on your disks. This lesson also contains fundamental information on how MS-DOS 5 uses different types of files and the procedures for naming them.

The Importance of Files

Whereas the DOS Shell's main function when working with disks is one of preparation (such as formatting), and its directory-related commands are designed primarily to promote organization, the real "grunt work" MS-DOS 5 was created to perform happens at the file level. Files exist at the very heart of your PC operations. They contain the instructions or information a PC requires to accomplish a specific task.

Different Types of Files

In general, PC files fall into two main categories:

- Program files.

- Data files.

You've already seen a few program files in action. For example, when you used the DOS Shell Format utility in Lesson 6, MS-DOS 5 actually loaded a program file called FORMAT.EXE into the memory installed in your PC. It then used the coded instructions contained on the program file to format the disk.

You've also encountered data files similar to the type that all PC programs rely on to work properly. When you formatted a system disk in Lesson 7, for example, you entered the command parameters **A:** **/S** in the DOS Shell Format dialog box. This information represented two pieces of data MS-DOS passed along to the FORMAT.EXE program as it was loaded, thus ensuring that your format operation would be performed precisely as you wanted it to be.

Sometimes, as was the case with a Format procedure, you can enter all the necessary data directly from the keyboard. More commonly, however, a program will read a second file, one containing the data it requires to run properly. This is especially true with powerful application programs (word processors, spreadsheets, database managers, and so on), which tend to use large amounts of data.

Application Program The term *application program* refers to a program that performs a specific function. A word processor, for example, is an application program used to enter and edit text on a personal computer.

MS-DOS File Naming Conventions

A DOS file name is divided into two parts:

- The file name, which identifies the specific contents of a file (for example, JDI-10, for a letter sent to John Dennis on January 10).

- An optional extension, which identifies the type of contents (for example, .LET for a letter).

In addition to this basic structure, the following rules govern the use of DOS file names:

1. The file name cannot exceed eight characters in length.

2. The extension portion can be no longer than three characters.

3. You use a period (.) to divide the file name from the extension.

4. You cannot include a blank space in either the file name or extension portion of a DOS file name.

5. You cannot use certain characters in a DOS file name, including

   . " / \ [ ] | < > + : = ; ,

Perhaps the most common convention employed when naming DOS files is to use the extension portion of the file name to indicate the contents of a specific file. For example, a .TXT extension is often used to indicate a text file, such as a document file for a word processor. One convention that borders on a strict rule is the fact that DOS recognizes files with an .EXE or .COM extension as being program files.

Viewing the File Listing

You'll perform most file-related operations from the *file listing* portion of the DOS Shell. This window, located just to the right of the Directory Tree in the middle of the DOS Shell screen, displays a listing of the files stored in the currently active directory. To see how the contents of the file listing window change as you move around a disk's directory structure:

- Click on the root directory (**C:**) in the Directory Tree.

Your screen should now resemble Figure 11-1, in which the file listing portion of the DOS Shell shows the files that Setup placed in the root directory during installation of MS-DOS 5.

```
                          MS-DOS Shell
    File  Options  View  Tree  Help
   C:\
   ⊟A   ⊟B   ▄C   ▄D

   ┌─ Directory Tree ─────────┐        C:\*.*
   │ ┌─ C\                  ↑│  ▤ AUTOEXEC.BAT      64  01-17-91 ↑
   │ ├── BATCH                │  ▤ COMMAND .COM  46,246  12-13-90
   │ ├── DOS                  │  ▤ CONFIG  .SYS      60  01-17-91
   │ └── OLD_DOS.1            │  ▤ WINA20  .386   9,349  12-13-90
   │                         ↓│                              ↓
   ├────────────── Disk Utilities ──────────────────────────────┐
   │ ▦ Main                  ↑
   │ ▤ Disk Copy                        Date last modified
   │ ▤ Backup Fixed Disk
   │ ▤ Restore Fixed Disk
   │ ▤ Quick Format
   │ ▤ Format
   │ ▤ Undelete              ↓
   └─────────────────────────────────────────────────────────────┘
   F10=Actions  Shift+F9=Command Prompt                  4:40 pm
```

Figure 11-1. The root directory file listing.

To make the root directory (**C:**) the active directory using the keyboard:

1. Press Tab until the Directory Tree becomes the active portion of your DOS Shell screen.

2. Use the arrow keys to position the highlight bar over the root directory listing (**C:**).

Something Old, Something New... Don't worry if the files listed in your display differ from those shown in Figure 11-1. The file listing here reflects the root directory of a system on which MS-DOS 5 was installed for the first time.

File listings consist of three columns, containing the following information:

• The file name and extension of each file.

• The size of the file, in bytes.

• A date, indicating when a file was last modified.

File Graphic Icons Some displays may show a graphic icon immediately to the left of the file name. When the DOS Shell is running in graphics mode, this icon indicates whether a file is a program file (a rectangular icon with a bar across the top) or a data file (a stylized sheet of paper with the top-right corner folded down).

Now, to view a different file listing:

• Click on the **DOS** directory in the directory tree.

Or

• Press the down-arrow key until the **DOS** directory is highlighted.

A completely different group of files should now be displayed in the file listing window, as illustrated in Figure 11-2. This new listing reflects the files stored in the DOS directory. Notice that a title bar at the top of the file listing window contains the name of the currently active directory.

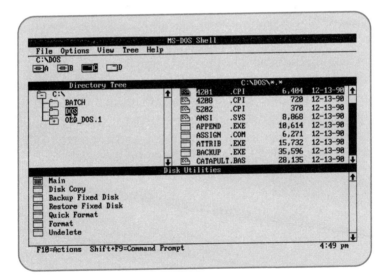

Figure 11-2. The contents of the file listing window reflecting your current position.

Accessing the File Listing

Once the desired group of files is displayed in the file listing, you'll need to access that portion of the DOS Shell screen in order to work with them. Use the following steps to make the file listing the active portion of your DOS Shell screen:

- Click on any file name in the file listing.

Or

- Press Tab.

In this lesson you've learned about the two different types of files that allow you to accomplish things with your PC. You've also learned the restrictions MS-DOS 5 places on naming files and how the file listing portion of the DOS Shell screen is used to display the files stored in the current directory. Finally, you learned how to make the file listing the active portion of the DOS Shell. In the next lesson you'll learn how to modify the appearance and contents of the DOS Shell file listing.

Lesson 12
Organizing the File Listing

In this lesson you'll learn how to request that only specific files be included in a file listing, along with the order in which they should appear.

Rearranging File Listings

The DOS Shell automatically displays every file stored in the active directory in alphabetical order, based on file name. If you'd rather see your files listed in a different order, you can use the following steps to change the order.

1. Select the directory from the Directory Tree (the DOS directory is used in the following exercise).

2. Click on any file name in the DOS file listing, or press Tab to activate the file listing.

3. Select Options in the menu bar.

4. Select File Display Options in the Options menu.

This calls up the Display Options dialog box shown in Figure 12-1. You use this dialog box to specify which files

69

you want your file listing to include. The dialog box in Figure 12-1 specifies all files, using the * wild-card character. (*.* means all file names and all extensions.)

Displays all files in directory

			MS-DOS Shell				

File Options View Tree Help
C:\DOS
▯A ▯B ▯C ▯D

Directory Tree   C:\DOS*.*
C:\
  BATCH   ↑ 4201   .CPI   6,404 12-13-90 ↑
  DOS   Display Options   12-13-90
  OLD_DOS   Name: ▮.▮   12-13-90
                                             12-13-90
                                             12-13-90
                               Sort by: 12-13-90
            [ ] Display hidden/system files ◉ Name   12-13-90
                                             ○ Extension 12-13-90 ↓
                                             ○ Date
  Main   [ ] Descending order   ○ Size   ↑
  Disk Copy   ○ DiskOrder
  Backup Fixe
  Restore Fix
  Quick Forma   (OK)   (Cancel)   (Help)
  Format
  Undelete

F10=Actions Shift+F9=Command Prompt   9:31 am

Figure 12-1. The Display Options dialog box.

You can also specify the order in which you want the files to appear. For example, you could use the following steps to organize the file listing in ascending order, by file size:

1. Click on the Size option in the Sort by: column.

2. Click on OK.

To sort your listing by file size directly from the keyboard

1. Press Tab three times to position the cursor in the Sort by: column.

2. Press the down-arrow key three times to activate the **Size** option.

3. Press Tab to position the cursor on the **OK** button.

4. Press Enter.

When you return to the DOS Shell, you'll notice that the order of your **DOS** directory file listing has changed to reflect the new sort preference, as shown in Figure 12-2.

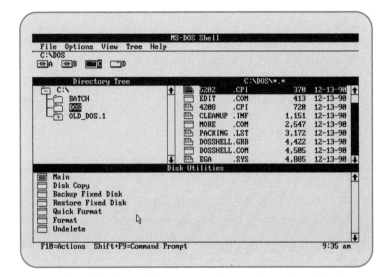

Figure 12-2. The directory listing sorted by file size.

Using DOS Wild Cards

Earlier, in the Display Options dialog box, you selected all files in the active directory by entering two asterisks separated by a period. The asterisks are *wild-card characters* that let you quickly select large groups of files. MS-DOS 5 supports two wild-card characters:

- When included in a file name, an asterisk (*) indicates that any characters can appear from that position on within the file's name or extension. For example, TEXT.* indicates any file with a file name portion of TEXT., regardless of its extension.

- When included in a file name, a question mark (?) indicates that any character can occupy that specific position. For example, TE?T.BAT would indicate either TEST.BAT, TEXT.BAT, or any other file matching this pattern, regardless of what character was in the third position.

You can use wild cards to identify groups of files with similar names. For example, you could use the following steps to list only those files in the DOS directory having a file extension of .EXE:

1. Select **Options** in the menu bar.

2. Select **File Display Options** in the Options menu.

3. When the Display Options dialog box appears, type *.EXE and press Enter or click on **OK**.

This time, when you return to the DOS Shell screen, the file listing will contain only EXE files, still sorted by file size, as shown in Figure 12-3.

Mix n' Match Combining both DOS wild-card characters within a single command is perfectly "legal." While this can get tricky, it does allow you to be quite explicit about the files you want used with a given DOS operation.

```
                          Secifies all files with an .EXE extension
                              MS-DOS Shell                   |
  File   Options   View   Tree   Help                        |
  C:\DOS                                                      |
  ⊡A  ⊡B  ■C  ⊟D                                             |
 ┌──── Directory Tree ──────────┬────── C:\DOS\*.EXE ───────────┐
 │ ⌐ C:\                      ↑ │ ▦ SORT    .EXE    6,618  12-13-90 ↑│
 │   ├─⌐ BATCH                  │ ▭ FIND    .EXE    6,642  12-13-90  │
 │   ├─⌐ DOS                    │ ▭ NLSFUNC .EXE    6,924  12-13-90  │
 │   └─⌐ OLD_DOS.1             │ ▭ EXE2BIN .EXE    8,360  12-13-90  │
 │                              │ ▭ LABEL   .EXE    8,954  12-13-90  │
 │                              │ ▭ RECOVER .EXE    9,098  12-13-90  │
 │                              │ ▭ SETVER  .EXE    9,162  12-13-90  │
 │                            ↓ │ ▭ APPEND  .EXE   10,614  12-13-90  │
 ├──────────── Disk Utilities ──│ ▭ SHARE   .EXE   10,768  12-13-90 ↓│
 │ ▦ Main                       │                                  ↑│
 │ ▭ Disk Copy                  │
 │ ▭ Backup Fixed Disk          │
 │ ▭ Restore Fixed Disk         │
 │ ▭ Quick Format               │
 │ ▭ Format                     │
 │ ▭ Undelete                   │                                  ↓│
 └ F10=Actions  Shift+F9=Command Prompt              9:52 am ──────┘
```

Figure 12-3. Using the DOS wild-card characters to specify certain files to be included in the file listing.

Before moving on, use the following steps to return the file listing to its default appearance—that is, including all files sorted by file name:

1. Select Options in the menu bar.

2. Select File Display Options in the Options menu.

3. When the Display Options dialog box appears, type *.*.

4. Select the Name option in the Sort by: column, (using the mouse or the Tab and up-arrow keys).

5. Click on OK, or press Enter.

Your file listing should now look as it did at the beginning of this lesson.

73

In this lesson you've learned how to change the contents and appearance of the DOS Shell file listings. You've also learned how to use the DOS wild-card characters to identify groups of files with similar names. In the next lesson you'll begin using this knowledge to copy and move files between different directory locations.

Lesson 13
Copying and Renaming Files

In this lesson you'll learn how to copy and rename files stored on your disks.

Copying Files

The DOS Shell makes copying files to a new disk or directory easy. Follow these steps to make a second copy of your AUTOEXEC.BAT file in the BATCH directory you created in an earlier lesson:

1. Click on the root directory listing (C:\) in the Directory Tree.

2. Point to the AUTOEXEC.BAT file in the file listing portion of the DOS Shell display.

3. Hold down the Ctrl key and the left mouse button.

4. Drag your mouse until the mouse pointer is positioned over the BATCH listing in the Directory Tree.

5. Release the Ctrl key and mouse button.

DOS Shell displays the Confirm Mouse Operation dialog box shown in Figure 13-1, asking you to verify that you want to perform the requested file copy. To complete the copy:

• Click on Yes.

```
                              MS-DOS Shell
    File  Options  View  Tree  Help
    C:\
    ⊟A  ⊟B  ▣C  ⊏D

       Directory Tree                  C:\*.*
    ⊟ C:\                    ↑ ▢ AUTOEXEC.BAT           64  01-17-91 ↑
      ⊟ BATCH           ┌── Confirm Mouse Operation ──┐ 46,246  12-13-90
      ⊟ DOS             │                             │     60  01-17-91
      ⊟ OLD_DOS.1       │  Are you sure you want to copy    9,349  12-13-90
                        │  the selected files to C:\BATCH?│
                        │                             │
                        │                             │
                        │   ▢ Yes ▢      ▢ No ▢       │
                        └─────────────────────────────┘           ↓
      ⊟ Command Prompt                                              ↑
      ⊟ Editor
      ⊟ MS-DOS QBasic
      ▦ Disk Utilities


    Copy AUTOEXEC.BAT to BATCH                              1:15 pm
```

Figure 13-1. Dragging your mouse with the Ctrl key depressed to copy files easily.

To initiate a copy operation directly from the keyboard:

1. Press Tab until the Directory Tree is the active window of your DOS Shell screen.

2. Use the arrow keys to highlight the root directory listing (**C:**).

3. Press Tab to make the file listing the active window of your DOS Shell screen.

4. Use the arrow keys to highlight the AUTOEXEC.BAT file.

5. Press Alt+F to display the File menu.

6. Press **C** to select **Copy**.

7. When the Copy File dialog box appears, type **C:\BATCH**.

8. Press Enter.

Either of these methods creates a duplicate copy of the AUTOEXEC.BAT file in the BATCH directory. Follow these steps to verify that the duplicate file was created:

1. Point to the BATCH directory listing in the Directory Tree.

2. Click the left mouse button to make this the active directory.

To select the BATCH directory directly from the keyboard:

1. Press Shift+Tab to make the Directory Tree the active window of your DOS Shell screen.

2. Use the down-arrow key to highlight **BATCH**.

You now have two files called AUTOEXEC.BAT on your disk: the one Setup originally created in the root directory and the new file you just placed in the BATCH directory. Duplicate file names could be confusing, however. The next section explains how to eliminate this potential problem.

One Key, No Waiting Copy is one example of a DOS Shell procedure that you can initiate with a single-key command, eliminating the need to access the File pull-down menu. After you select the file you want to copy, press F8 to display the Copy File dialog box immediately.

When working directly from the system prompt, you can use the MS-DOS 5 **COPY** command to copy a file to a different disk or directory.

Renaming a File

The DOS Shell **Rename** option enables you to change the name of a file without modifying that file's contents. Use the following steps, for example, to rename the AUTOEXEC.BAT file in the BATCH directory to AUTOEXEC.HLD:

1. Click on **AUTOEXEC.BAT** in the file listing for the BATCH directory.

2. Click on **File** in the DOS Shell menu bar.

3. Click on the **Rename** option.

This displays the Rename File dialog box shown in Figure 13-2. Use this dialog box to specify a new name for the selected file.

To display the Rename File dialog box directly from the keyboard:

1. Press Tab to activate the Directory Tree window of your DOS Shell screen and highlight **AUTOEXEC.BAT**.

2. Press Alt+F to display the File menu.

3. Press **N** to select **Rename**.

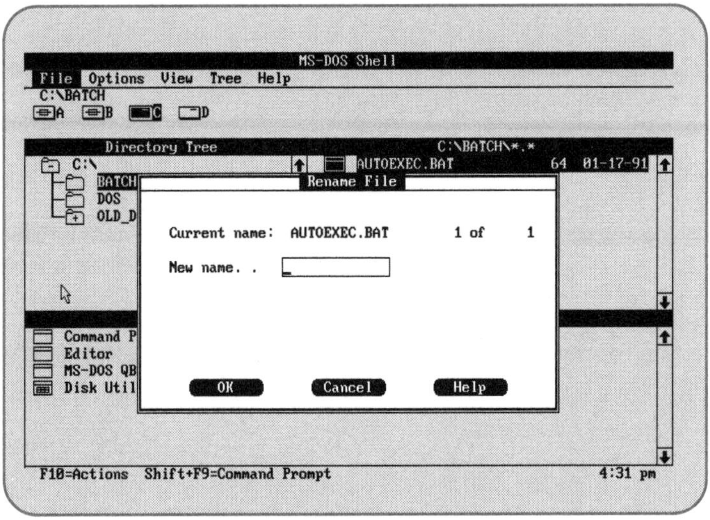

Figure 13-2. The Rename File dialog box.

Use the following steps to rename AUTOEXEC.BAT to AUTOEXEC.HLD:

- Type **AUTOEXEC.HLD** and select **OK**.

Or

- Type **AUTOEXEC.HLD** and press Enter.

MS-DOS 5 renames the file and returns you to the DOS Shell screen. Notice that the new file name now appears in the file listing for the BATCH directory.

Familiarity Breeds Contentment The .HLD extension is often used to identify a "hold" file—that is, a file that you want to save for one reason or another. In this case, your goal is to preserve the contents of your original AUTOEXEC.BAT file in case you ever need to refer to that file and see how MS-DOS 5 initially configured your system.

When working directly from the system prompt, you can use the MS-DOS 5 **REN** (Rename) command to rename files.

In this lesson you've learned how to copy and rename a file. In the next lesson you'll learn how to move files from within the DOS Shell.

Lesson 14
Moving Files

In this lesson you'll learn how to move files stored on your disks.

Relocating a File

In the preceding lesson, renaming AUTOEXEC.HLD eliminated the confusion of having multiple files with the same name on your disk. However, this left the "reserve" copy of your AUTOEXEC.BAT file stored in a location different from the original, and having these two files in the same directory would make more sense. To move AUTOEXEC.HLD from your BATCH directory back to the root directory of drive C:

1. Point to the file you want to move, in this case the **AUTOEXEC.HLD** file in the BATCH directory file listing. Hold down the left mouse button.

2. Drag your mouse until the mouse pointer is positioned over the directory that you want to move the file to, in this case the root directory (**C:**) listing in the Directory Tree.

3. Release the left mouse button.

DOS Shell displays the Confirm Mouse Operation dialog box shown in Figure 14-1. This dialog box is almost identical to the one in Figure 13-1, except that it asks you to verify that you want to move, rather than copy, the selected file. To complete the move:

• Click on Yes.

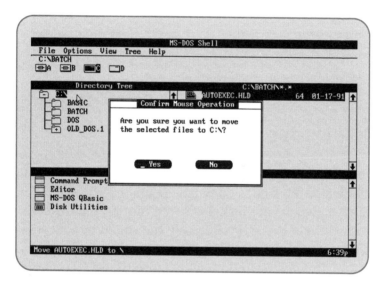

Figure 14-1. Dragging your mouse with the left button depressed to copy files easily.

To initiate a Move operation directly from the keyboard:

1. Highlight the file you want to move, in this case, the **AUTOEXEC.HLD** file.

2. Press Alt+F to access the File menu.

3. Press **M** to select **Move**.

4. When the Move File dialog box appears, type the directory that you want to move the file to, in this case, **C:**.

5. Press Enter.

The **AUTOEXEC.HLD** file disappears from the BATCH directory file listing. Follow these steps to verify that the file moved to its new location:

1. Point to the root directory listing (**C:**) in the Directory Tree.

2. Click the left mouse button to make this the active directory.

   To check the contents of the root directory from the keyboard:

   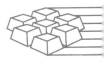

   • Use the arrow keys to highlight the root directory listing (**C:**).

Notice that the new file name appears directly below AUTOEXEC.BAT. The DOS Shell automatically placed AUTOEXEC.HLD in the correct alphabetical position, based on its file name, within the directory listing. Lesson 12 gives instructions on how to change the order in which the DOS Shell organizes its file listings.

   There is no single MS-DOS 5 command that corresponds to a DOS Shell Move operation. If you're working from the system prompt. Follow this two-step procedure:

   1. Copy the file to its new location using the MS-DOS 5 **COPY** command.

2. Then use a **DEL** command to delete the original.

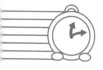

Second Shortcut Move is another DOS Shell procedure that has a corresponding single-key shortcut. After selecting the file you want to move, press F7 to display the Move File dialog box.

In this lesson you've learned how to move a file. In the next lesson you'll learn how to select multiple files and copy or move them in a single operation.

Lesson 15
Searching for Files with Similar Names

In this lesson you'll learn how to use the DOS Shell **Search** option to select multiple files, which you can then copy or move to a new location.

Using the Search Option

You can use File Search with other DOS Shell procedures to transform otherwise complicated activities into relatively simple tasks. For example, you can use the Search and Copy function to quickly copy all QBasic data files shipped with MS-DOS 5 to a dedicated BASIC direc̶t̶o̶r̶y̶. To prepare for the exercises in this lesson, ̶f̶o̶l̶l̶o̶w̶ ̶t̶h̶e̶s̶e̶ steps to create a directory named BA̶S̶I̶C̶.

1. Select the root directory (**C:**) in ̶t̶h̶e̶

2. Select **File** in the DOS Shell menu.

3. Select the **Create Directory** option.

4. When the Create Directory dialog bo̶x̶ ̶a̶p̶p̶e̶a̶r̶s̶,̶ ̶t̶y̶p̶e̶ **BASIC** and press Enter.

This creates a first-level subdirectory called BASIC, running off the root directory. Now, use the following steps to find all files with a particular extension (in this case, .BAS) and combine them into a single directory:

1. Click on **File** in the DOS Shell menu bar.

2. Click on the **Search** option.

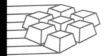

To begin a Search operation directly from the keyboard:

1. Press Alt+F to display the File pull-down menu.

2. Press **H** to select **Search**.

This displays the Search File dialog box shown in Figure 15-1. You use this dialog box to specify what files Search should look for, along with how comprehensive this search should be.

```
                        MS-DOS Shell
 File Options  View  Tree  Help
   C:\
  ⊟A  ⊟B  ▆▆C  ⊑D

        Directory Tree                          C:\*.*
                            ┌──── Search File ──────────┐   64  01-17-91 ↑
  ⊟ C:\                     │          Search File       │   64  01-17-91
   ⊢⊠ BAS                   │                           │46,246 12-13-90
   ⊢⊟ BAT │ Current Directory is C:\          │           60  01-17-91
   ⊢⊟ DOS │                           │        9,349  12-13-90
   ⊢⊞ OLD │ Search for. .  ▓▓▓          │
         │      [X] Search entire disk      │
         │                           │
         │  ┌── OK ──┐   ┌─Cancel─┐  ┌─Help─┐ │
  ⊟ Command│  └────────┘   └────────┘  └──────┘ │
  ⊟ Editor └──────────────────────────┘
  ⊟ MS-DOS QBasic        Tells DOS to search for all files
  ▦ Disk Utilities


                                            7:13 pm
 F10=Actions  Shift+F9=Command Prompt
```

Figure 15-1. The Search File dialog box.

86

Once this dialog box is displayed, use the following steps to find all files with a .BAS extension on drive C:

1. Type *.BAS.

2. Press Enter.

MS-DOS 5 scans your entire hard disk and then displays a Search Results screen containing a list of all files with the specified extension, as shown in Figure 15-2.

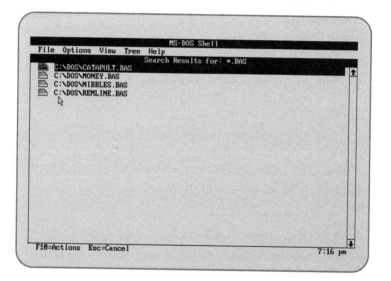

Figure 15-2. The Search Results screen.

Wild Things Remember, the MS-DOS 5 wild-card characters allow you to quickly identify files with similar file names. In this example, you used the asterisk (*) wild-card character to specify all files with a .BAS extension.

Working With Search Results

Once a Search Results list exists, you can use additional DOS Shell options to manage the files it contains. For example, use the following steps to select all the files located by the Search operation:

1. Click on **File** in the DOS Shell menu bar.

2. Click on the **Select All** option.

 To select all files located by a Search operation directly from the keyboard:

    1. Press Alt+F to display the File pull-down menu.

    2. Press S to select **Select All**.

When the DOS Shell screen returns, all the files on the Search Results screen are highlighted, as shown in Figure 15-3.

After all the BAS files have been selected, you can use the mouse or keyboard to move them easily to the BASIC directory:

1. Select **File** from the DOS Shell menu bar.

2. Select the **Move** option from the File pull-down menu.

3. At the Move File dialog box, type **C:\BASIC**.

4. Click on **OK** or press Enter.

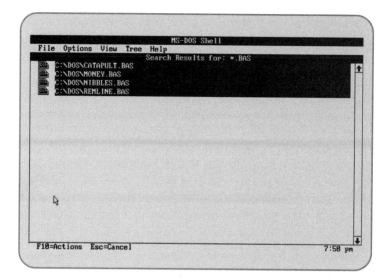

Figure 15-3. Using the Select All option to quickly mark all files located in a Search operation.

This moves all BAS files currently stored on your hard disk to the BASIC directory. Use the following steps to verify the results:

1. Click on **View** in the DOS Shell menu.

2. Click on **Program/File Lists** on the View pull-down menu.

3. When the DOS Shell displays, click on the **BASIC** directory in the Directory Tree.

> To verify the results of a move from the keyboard:
>
> 1. Press Esc to remove the Search Results screen.

2. Press Shift+Tab or Tab to make the Directory Tree the active window of your DOS Shell screen if it is not active.

3. Use the appropriate arrow keys to highlight the **BASIC** directory.

Your screen should now resemble Figure 15-4, which shows the file listing for the BASIC directory. Notice that only the files located in the previous Search—that is, files with a .BAS extension—were duplicated on this disk during the Copy procedure.

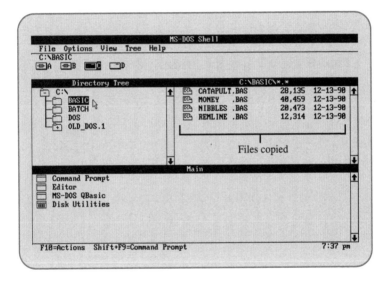

Figure 15-4. Simplifying potentially complicated procedures with the DOS Shell Search option.

Some additional activities that you can simplify using the **Search** option include:

- Deleting all files with matching file name extensions.

• Copying all data files relating to a given project to a single directory or archive disk (if you applied a standard naming convention to these files as you created them).

• Moving all files with a .BAT extension into a dedicated batch-file directory.

In this lesson you've learned how you can use the DOS Shell **Search** option to identify files with similar file names. You also learned to use the **Select All** option to mark the resulting file list for additional processing. In the next lesson you'll learn how to delete and undelete files.

Deleting and Undeleting Files

In this lesson you'll learn how to delete files stored on your disks from within the DOS Shell. You'll also learn how to use the Undelete utility to recover accidentally deleted files.

Deleting Files

Deleting files is as potentially destructive as it is useful because it's so easy to do. For example, you can use the following steps to delete from your root directory the AUTOEXEC.HLD file created in Lesson 13:

1. Click on or highlight the root directory listing (**C:**) in the Directory Tree.

2. Click on or highlight the **AUTOEXEC.HLD** file in the file listing window of the DOS Shell screen.

3. Select **File** in the DOS Shell menu bar.

4. Select **Delete** in the File pull-down menu.

DOS Shell displays the Delete File Confirmation dialog box shown in Figure 16-1, asking you to verify that you want to delete the selected file. Click on **Yes** or press Enter to erase AUTOEXEC.HLD.

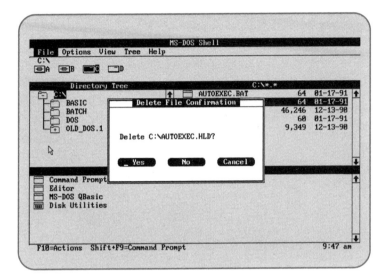

Figure 16-1. The Delete File Confirmation dialog box.

One-button Bye-Bye Delete is another DOS Shell procedure with a corresponding single-key shortcut. After selecting the file(s) you want to erase, press the Del key to display the Delete File Confirmation dialog box.

When working directly from the system prompt, you can use the MS-DOS 5 **DEL** (Delete) command to erase unwanted files.

Recovering Deleted Files

If you accidentally delete a file that you want to keep, try the Undelete feature. For example, use the following steps to recover the AUTOEXEC.HLD file deleted in the previous exercise:

1. Select **Disk Utilities** in the Main program group at the bottom of your DOS Shell screen.

2. Select **Undelete** in the resulting list of Disk Utilities options.

   This displays the Undelete dialog box shown in Figure 16-2.

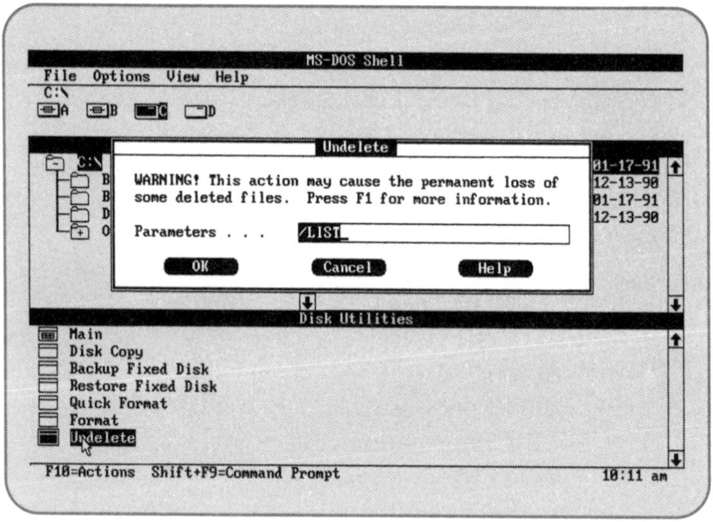

Figure 16-2. The Undelete dialog box.

If you know the name of the file you want to restore, type it directly into this dialog box and press Enter. If not, accept the default /LIST parameter by clicking on **OK** or pressing Enter. MS-DOS 5 will display a list of recently deleted files that may be recoverable, as shown in Figure 16-3. In this instance, the list indicates that you can recover one file, **?UTOEXEC.HLD.**

```
Directory: C:\
File Specs: *.*

    Delete Tracking file not found.

    MS-DOS Directory contains    1 deleted files.
    Of those,    1 files may be recovered.

Using the MS-DOS Directory.

    ?UTOEXEC HLD        64  1-17-91 10:01p  ...A
                                                    ──── Recoverable file
Press any key to return to MS-DOS Shell....
```

Figure 16-3. Using the /LIST parameter to determine whether any files in the current directory can be "undeleted."

This odd-looking file name reflects how MS-DOS 5 keeps track of files. When you delete a file, DOS does not actually erase all the data that file contains. Rather, MS-DOS modifies its disk directory by replacing the first character of that file's name with a question mark. Then, DOS frees up the portions of the disk previously occupied by this file to store other data, if needed. The leading question mark tells DOS to no longer display this file in its directory listings. If you make an attempt soon enough, you may be able to recover an erased file. To actually undelete AUTOEXEC.HLD:

1. Press any key to exit the Undelete file list.

2. Double-click on Undelete or use the arrow keys to highlight it and press Enter.

3. When the Undelete dialog box appears, type ?UTOEXEC.HLD and press Enter.

MS-DOS 5 displays a screen similar to Figure 16-3, but with the message Do you want to undelete this file? (Y/N). To instruct MS-DOS 5 to undelete ?UTOEXEC.HLD, press **Y**.

Finally, MS-DOS 5 asks what it should use as the first character in the file name of the restored file. (Remember, DOS replaced the original "A" with a question mark. To have MS-DOS 5 place an **A** at the beginning of the restored file, press **A**.)

DOS responds with a message indicating whether the undelete was successful. To return to the DOS Shell screen, press any key.

Even after a successful undelete operation, the restored file still may not show up on your directory. DOS Shell merely redisplays the last directory listing it has access to—one lacking the restored file. Use the following steps to refresh the DOS Shell display to include the restored file:

1. Activate the Directory Tree.

2. Select View in the DOS Shell menu bar.

3. Select Refresh in the View pull-down menu.

When working directly from the system prompt, you can use the MS-DOS 5 **UNDELETE** command to recover erased files.

In this lesson you've learned how to delete files from your DOS disks. You also learned how the MS-DOS 5 Undelete utility allows you to recover accidentally erased files. In the next lesson you'll learn how to view and change the contents of a file using the **View File Contents** option and the MS-DOS Editor.

Viewing and Changing the Contents of a File

In this lesson you'll learn how to use the DOS Shell **View File Contents** option to display a file on-screen. You'll also learn how you can use the MS-DOS 5 Editor to modify a file's contents by adding the BATCH directory to a PATH statement in your AUTOEXEC.BAT file.

Viewing a File

The DOS Shell **View File Contents** option enables you to display the actual contents of a file on-screen. Unless you are an experienced programmer, this capability is of only minimal value for program files. However, even newcomers to MS-DOS can learn something by viewing the contents of a text file—especially when that file is used to tell your computer to do something, as is the case with the AUTOEXEC.BAT file.

AUTOEXEC.BAT is a special file that MS-DOS 5 looks for each time you start your PC. If AUTOEXEC.BAT exists, DOS automatically executes any commands it contains, before turning control of your system over to you. (Remember: AUTOEXEC is an acronym for "AUTOmatic

EXECution.") As a rule, Setup creates an initial AUTOEXEC.BAT file for your PC during installation of MS-DOS 5. Use the following steps to view the contents of your AUTOEXEC.BAT file:

1. Select the root directory (C:\) of your Directory Tree.

2. Select **AUTOEXEC.BAT** in the file listing.

3. Select **File** from the DOS Shell menu bar.

4. Select **View File Contents**.

The **View File Contents** option allows you to view the contents of a selected file on-screen. At this point, your screen should resemble Figure 17-1, which shows the contents of one AUTOEXEC.BAT file created by Setup during installation of MS-DOS 5.

```
                         MS-DOS Shell - AUTOEXEC.BAT
  Display  View  Help
     To view file's content use ▨▨▨ or ▨▨▨ or ↑ or ↓.

  @ECHO OFF
  PROMPT $p$g
  PATH C:\DOS
  SET TEMP=C:\DOS
  DOSSHELL

      ↖



  ←┘=PageDown  Esc=Cancel  F9=Hex/ASCII                      1:09 pm
```

Figure 17-1. The contents of an AUTOEXEC.BAT file.

A Very Personal File Your AUTOEXEC.BAT file may differ from the one shown in Figure 17-1. The exact contents of AUTOEXEC.BAT depend on the results of the analysis Setup performed on your PC when it first installed MS-DOS 5. This figure reflects the results of installing MS-DOS 5 on a relatively simple PC system.

A PATH statement, one of the commands in AUTOEXEC.BAT, allows DOS to find and execute programs stored in a location other than the currently active directory. For example, because Setup automatically created a path to the DOS directory, you can use the DOS Shell without having to change to that directory each time you want to run an MS-DOS 5 program. Modifying AUTOEXEC.BAT to include more directories in the path statement is easy. Before doing this, however, you need to exit the **View File Contents** option and return to the DOS Shell, using the following steps:

1. Select **View** from the menu bar.

2. Select **Restore View**.

When working directly from the system prompt, you can use the MS-DOS 5 **TYPE** command to view the contents of a file.

Starting the MS-DOS 5 Editor

Editor is one of the options in the Main program group. Use the following steps to start Editor:

1. If the Disk Utilities program group is still active, select the **Main** option.

2. Select **Editor** in the Main program group.

This displays the File to Edit dialog box shown in Figure 17-2, requesting the name of the file you want to edit.

1. Type **AUTOEXEC.BAT**.

2. Press Enter.

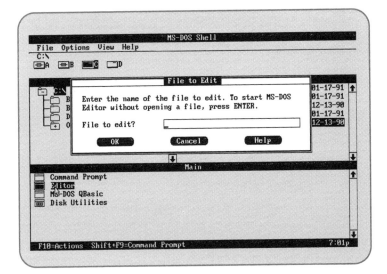

Figure 17-2. The File to Edit dialog box.

DOS Shell starts Editor, loads your AUTOEXEC.BAT file, and displays the opening screen shown in Figure 17-3. This screen contains a menu bar, similar to the one found in the DOS Shell. It also has a status line running across the bottom of the screen.

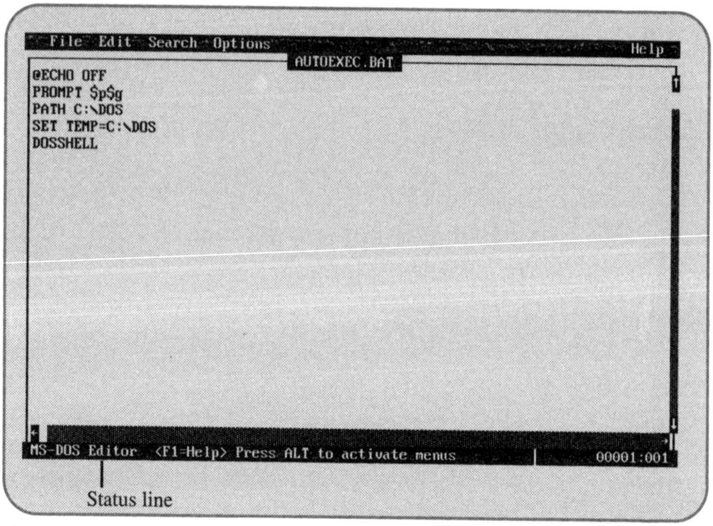

Figure 17-3. The Editor with screen elements similar to the DOS Shell.

Editing AUTOEXEC.BAT

To edit the contents of a file with Editor, you simply position the cursor where you want to make your changes and type them. For example, you could use the following steps to add your BATCH directory to the current PATH statement:

1. Use the arrow keys to position the cursor at the end of the line that currently reads: `PATH C:\DOS`.

2. Type **;C:\BATCH**.

This inserts the specified text immediately following the DOS path in the original statement. The MS-DOS 5 documentation contains additional information about commands that can be used in an AUTOEXEC.BAT file, including the PATH statement.

Saving an Edited File

Use the following steps to save the modified AUTOEXEC.BAT file back to disk so that the changes you made will take effect the next time you start your PC:

1. Select File from the menu bar.

2. Select Save.

   Editor saves the changes to disk and returns you to its text-editing screen.

Exiting Editor

After you've saved your new file, you can use the following steps to exit the Editor and return to the DOS Shell:

1. Select File from the menu bar.

2. Select Exit.

   This ends the current Editor session and returns you to the DOS Shell. If you are working in Editor and need assistance with a specific procedure, click on on-line Help or press Alt-H.

   In this lesson you've learned how to view and modify text files. Specifically, you used Editor to modify AUTOEXEC.BAT and change the way MS-DOS 5 sets itself up during system startup. In the next lesson you'll learn how to create your own program groups within the DOS Shell.

Creating Program Groups

In this lesson you'll learn how to set up program groups in the DOS Shell.

Program Groups

You've already used the DOS Shell in preceding lessons to access programs and utilities. These include:

- Command prompt

- Editor

- MS-DOS QBasic

- Disk Utilities

To take full advantage of the DOS Shell, however, you need to learn how to include your favorite application programs in the program group window of the DOS Shell screen. You'll also learn how to run the application programs you'll use regularly on your PC.

Creating a New Program Group

To create a program group, the Program Group window must be the active window of your DOS Shell screen.

- Click on **Command Prompt** in the Program Group window.

Or

- Press Tab until the highlight bar is located in the Program Group window.

After the Program Group window is active, you can use the following steps to create a new program group:

1. Select **File** from the DOS Shell menu bar.

2. Select **New**.

This displays the New Program Object dialog box shown in Figure 18-1. Follow these steps to tell DOS Shell that you are creating a new group:

1. Select **Program Group**.

2. Select **OK**.

This displays the Add Group dialog box shown in Figure 18-2. You use this dialog box to assign a title to your new program group. The name you enter in the Title field will appear in the Main program group window of your DOS Shell. Optional items specified with the Add Group dialog box include:

```
                        MS-DOS Shell
  File Options View Help
  C:\BATCH
  [A  [B  [C  [D

  [ C:\     ┌──────── New Program Object ────────┐ BATCH\*.*
                                                       64  01-17-91
           ┌ New ────────────────────────┐
           │  ○  Program Group      ▐ OK ▌│
           │  ◉  Program Item    ▐ Cancel ▌│
           └──────────────────────────────┘
                            ↓
                           Main
  Command Prompt
  Editor
  MS-DOS QBasic
  Disk Utilities

  F10=Actions  Shift+F9=Command Prompt                 10:46 pm
```

Figure 18-1. Using the New Program Object dialog box to supply information about your new program group.

- **Help Text**—In this field you can type a Help message, up to 256 characters long, which the DOS Shell will display when you access on-line Help for this program group.

- **Password**—In this field you can type a password that later you will need to enter before you can access this program group.

Short Is Sweet Program group names can be up to 74 characters long. Keeping group names short, however, conserves space on your DOS Shell screen.

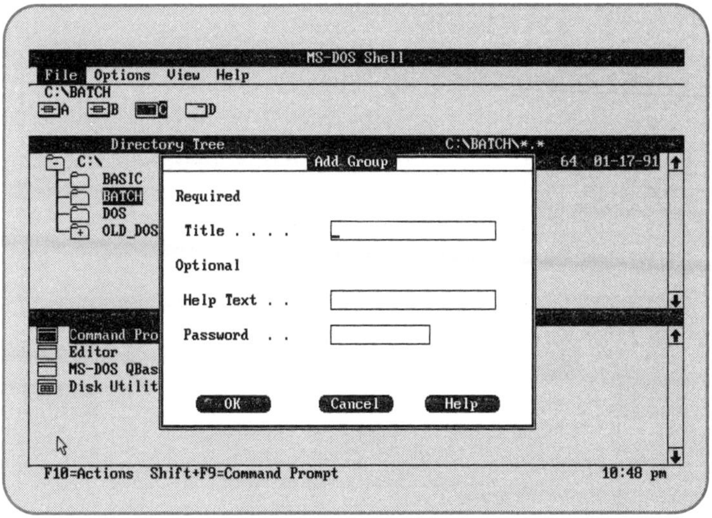

Figure 18-2. The Add Group dialog box.

Use the following steps to assign a name to a new program group:

1. Type the group name (in this example, **Misc. Utilities**).

2. Press Enter or click on **OK**.

Adding Items to a Program Group

A new listing, `Misc. Utilities`, has been added to the Program Group window. Once a group exists, you can use the following steps to add items to it:

1. Select **Misc. Utilities**.

2. Select **File** from the DOS Shell menu bar.

3. Select **New**.

4. Click on **OK** or press Enter.

This displays the Add Program dialog box shown in Figure 18-3, which you use to specify the information MS-DOS 5 will need to run this item whenever you select it from your Misc. Utilities group.

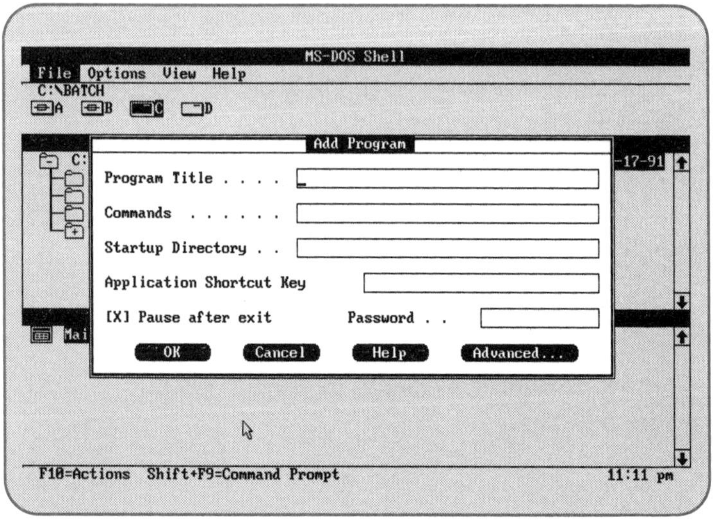

Figure 18-3. The Add Program dialog box.

Use the following steps to add an item to your Misc. Utilities program group that will report on the current status of your PC's memory:

1. Type **Check Memory** and press Tab.

2. Type **MEM.EXE** and press Tab.

3. Type **C:\DOS** and press Tab.

4. Press Enter or click on **OK**.

MS-DOS adds a new item identified as Check Memory to your Misc. Utilities program group. Then it returns you to the DOS Shell.

Selecting a Program Group Item

If everything is in place, select **Check Memory** in the Misc. Utilities program window. This runs MEM.EXE, an MS-DOS 5 utility program that analyzes your PC's memory and returns information on the memory available.

Notice that MS-DOS 5 temporarily suspended execution after running MEM.EXE and displayed the following message:

```
Press any key to return to MS-DOS Shell
```

This occurred because you left the **Pause after exit** option active in the Add Program dialog box for Check Memory. Specify this option whenever a program you're executing from the DOS Shell program manager displays information you want to read before returning to the DOS Shell.

Modifying a Program Group Item

Modifying an already existing Program Group item is possible. Suppose, for example, that you want to provide on-line assistance for someone who may not know what Check Memory does. Use the following steps to create an on-line Help message for Check Memory:

1. Select **File** from the DOS Shell menu bar.

2. Select **Properties**.

3. When the Program Item Properties dialog box appears, select **Advanced**.

This displays the Advanced dialog box shown in Figure 18-4. You use this dialog box to specify information for a program group item that already exists. (This book concentrates only on the Help Text field.)

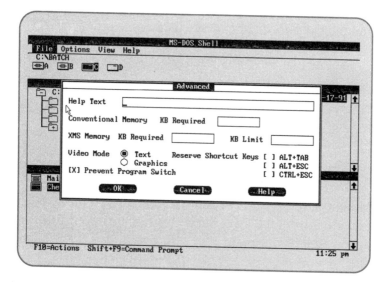

Figure 18-4. The Advanced Properties dialog box.

Use this field to create a Help message, up to 256 characters long, which the DOS Shell will display when you access on-line Help for this program item.

1. Move to the Help field.

2. Type **Use this utility to check the current status of the memory installed on your PC**.

3. Press Enter or click on **OK** to return to the Program Item Properties dialog box.

4. Press Enter or click on **OK** to accept your modifications.

Use the following steps to see what MS-DOS 5 did with your Help message:

1. If necessary, highlight **Check Memory** in the Program Group window.

2. Press F1.

This displays the MS-DOS Shell Help window shown in Figure 18-5, containing the message specified in the preceding exercise.

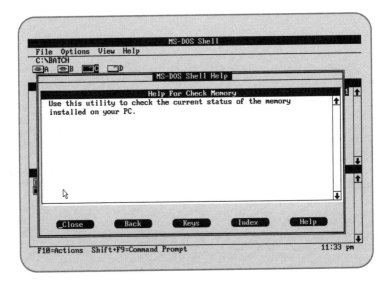

Figure 18-5. An on-line Help message for your program group options.

To remove this message from the screen:

- Point to **Close** and click the left mouse button, or press Esc.

In this lesson you've learned how to create and manage program groups and add your favorite application programs to the DOS Shell environment. In the next lesson you'll learn how to use the DOS Shell's built-in task swapper.

Running Multiple Programs in the DOS Shell

In this lesson you'll learn how to use the DOS Shell Task Swapper to manage multiple application programs running concurrently under MS-DOS 5. You'll also learn how to use the **Run** option to open applications from within the DOS Shell.

What Is Task Swapping?

Beginning with MS-DOS 5, Microsoft is adding a powerful new feature to the DOS Shell: task swapping. Task swapping enables you to load more than one application program at the same time and switch between them quickly, all from within the DOS Shell.

For example, you use one program (writing a letter with your word processor, for instance) and switch to a second program (a financial program or electronic spreadsheet, to record your mortgage payment) without completely closing down the first program. After you've completed the second task, you can use the Active Task List to return to your word processing program and continue your letter, exactly where you left off.

Enabling the Task Swapper

In its default configuration, the DOS Shell does not support task swapping. Before you can take advantage of this feature, you must enable it.

1. Select **Options** from the DOS Shell menu bar.

2. Select **Enable Task Swapper.**

This adds a new window marked Active Task List to your DOS Shell screen, as shown in Figure19-1.

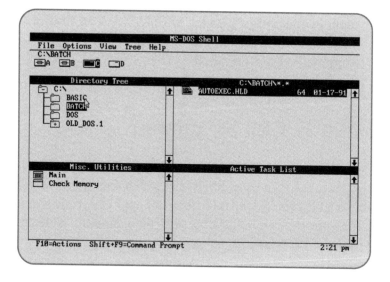

Figure 19-1. Adding an Active Task List window to the DOS Shell screen.

Adding a Program to the Task List

When you activate the Active Task List, it contains no program names. To add an application to the Active Task List, you must run it from within the DOS Shell. You can accomplish this in one of four ways:

- Using the **Run** option on the File menu.

- Double-clicking on that program's file name within the directory listing.

- Double-clicking on a data file that has been associated with the application you want to run.

- Double-clicking on a program group item corresponding to the application you want to run.

For example, follow these steps to open the MS-DOS 5 Editor with task swapping enabled using the **Run** option:

1. Highlight the DOS directory in the Directory Tree.

2. Select File from the DOS Shell menu bar.

3. Select Run from the File pull-down menu.

Selecting **Run** displays the dialog box shown in Figure 19-2. To run an application from this dialog box, enter the DOS command normally used to start that program at the Command Line prompt. For example, to start the DOS Shell Editor:

1. Type EDIT.

2. Press Enter or click on OK.

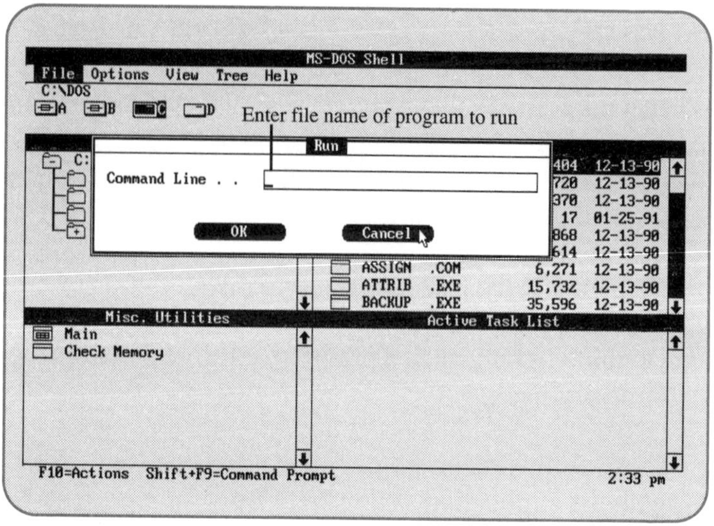

Figure 19-2. The Run dialog box.

After a few seconds, you will see the MS-DOS Editor "welcome" message. To remove this opening message and advance to the text editing screen, press Esc. To leave Editor active and return to the DOS Shell:

* Press Alt+Tab.

Notice that an item marked EDIT has been added to the Active Task List window, as shown in Figure 19-3.

Alt+Tab switches between multiple programs running in a task swapping session. Because Edit is the only program currently open, Alt+Tab returns you to the DOS Shell. Pressing Alt+Tab cycles you through any open applications in a "round-robin" fashion.

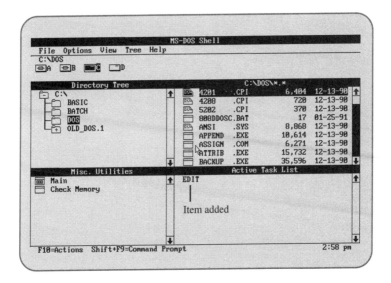

Figure 19-3. Starting a program with task swapping to add that program automatically to the Task List.

Adding a Second Program to the Task List

Now, use another method of running a program to add a program called Money Manager to the Task List:

1. Highlight **BASIC** on the Directory Tree.

2. Select **MONEY.BAS** in the file listing window of the DOS Shell screen.

After a few seconds, you'll see the opening message for Money Manager, a personal financial management program shipped with MS-DOS 5. To remove this message and start Money Manager, press any key.

117

Press Alt+Tab to return to the DOS Shell. Notice that a second program listing, MONEY.BAS, has been added to the Active Task List, as shown in Figure 19-4.

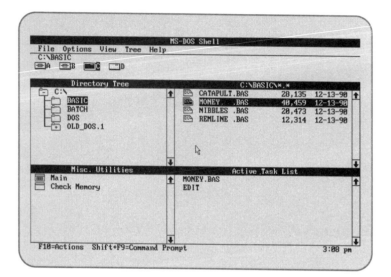

Figure 19-4. Including additional programs to run during a task-swapping session in the Active Task List.

Removing Programs from the Task List

The safest way to remove an application from the Active Task List is to make that application the active program and then close it down as though it were running under standard DOS. Doing so automatically removes that application from your current Task List.

There may be times, however, when you will be forced to manually delete applications from the Active Task List. This method is not recommended but might be required, for example, if a program "freezes"—that is, fails unexpectedly—during a task swapping session. For example, use the following steps to manually delete Money Manager from the Task List:

1. Select **MONEY.BAS** in the Task List window.

2. Select **File** from the DOS Shell menu bar.

3. Select **Delete**.

DOS displays a warning message similar to the one shown in Figure 19-5. As this message states, you should use this method to modify your Active Task List only as a last resort—that is, if all other attempts to quit the program in the normal fashion fail.

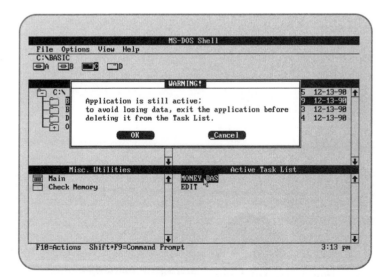

Figure 19-5. A WARNING! message box.

To finish removing Money Manager from the Active Task List, select **OK**.

Start With a Clean Slate If you are forced to remove a problematic application from the Active Task List with the **Delete** option, you should immediately close any other open programs currently in the Active Task List (using their normal exit procedures), leave the DOS Shell, and then reboot your system. Doing so eliminates the possibility of problems later in your task swapping session.

Task swapping is a powerful and potentially useful feature. Keep in mind, however, that using such an advanced procedure as the DOS 5.0 Active Task List can be tricky. Experiment with the DOS 5.0 Task List before incorporating it into your day-to-day PC operations. For now, use the following steps to close Editor:

1. Press Alt+Tab to switch to Editor.

2. Press Alt+F to display the Editor File menu.

3. Press **X** to select **Exit**.

4. When the `Press any key to return to MS-DOS Shell` message appears, press any key.

This returns you to the DOS Shell. The empty Active Task List window indicates that no applications are running in the current session.

In this lesson you've learned about the Task Swapper, a new feature of MS-DOS 5 that provides quick access to several programs running under the DOS Shell. In the next lesson you'll learn how to protect your files using the Backup Fixed Disk utility.

Lesson 20
The Backup Fixed Disk Utility

In this lesson you'll learn how to use the Backup Fixed Disk utility to protect your files.

Archiving Disk Files (The Backup Utility)

Hard disks, the mass storage media of choice among PC users, sometimes fail. The potential loss of data associated with such a failure is avoidable, thanks to the DOS Shell Backup Fixed Disk utility. You use the Backup Fixed Disk utility to make archival copies of the files stored on your hard disk. As a rule, you create these copies on floppy disks, which you can then safely store away and have readily available if you ever need to reconstruct a damaged file or, in a worst-case scenario, recover all the files from a damaged hard disk.

Starting the Backup Utility

Use the following steps with the mouse or keyboard to start the DOS Shell Backup Fixed Disk utility:

1. Select **Disk Utilities** from the Main program group.

2. Select **Backup Fixed Disk.**

This displays the Backup Fixed Disk dialog box shown in Figure 20-1. You use this dialog box to instruct MS-DOS 5 on how the current backup operation should be performed. Although it will work on any disk type, the Backup utility is most commonly employed to archive the large numbers of files associated with using a hard disk.

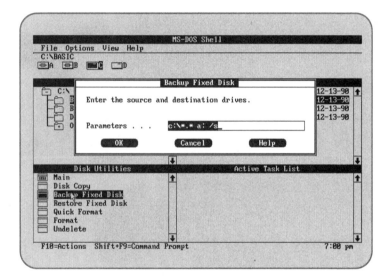

Figure 20-1. The Backup Fixed Disk dialog box.

Backup Fixed Disk Dialog Box Syntax

You can use the Backup Fixed Disk dialog box to record relatively complicated instructions easily. Enter parameters into the Backup Fixed Disk dialog box using the following format:

[drive1:] [path] [filename] [drive2] [command option]

Where:

- *drive1* is the drive letter of the disk containing the file(s) to be backed up (**C:** in Figure 20-1).

- *path* is the name of a directory or subdirectory containing the files you want to archive (\, the root directory, in Figure 20-1).

- *filename* is the name of any files you want to archive, which can include wild-card characters to specify multiple files (***.***, or all files, in Figure 20-1).

- *drive2* is the target drive—that is, the drive containing the disk(s) on which you want the specified file(s) to be archived (**a:** in Figure 20-1).

- *command option* is one or more of the Backup options described in the next section (**/s** in Figure 20-1).

Refer to Lesson 21 for examples using the Backup utility.

Backup Options

The Backup utility supports several options, which can be used to specify which files on *drive1* should be archived and how they should be stored on *drive2*. Command options supported by the Backup utility are shown in Table 20-1.

Table 20-1. Backup Utility Options

Options	Function
/s	Backs up any subdirectories associated with the specified path
/m	Backs up only those files that have been altered since the previous backup
/a	Appends any files being archived with the current BACKUP operation to those already stored on the backup disks
/d:date	Archives only those files that have been modified on or after the specified date
/t:time	Archives only those files that have been modified since the specified time
/L:filename	Creates a log file called filename, in which a record of the current backup operation is stored
/f:size	Causes the target disk in drive2 to be formatted to the specified size, if necessary, prior to the actual backup being performed. (The **/f:** option is only available in DOS versions 3.3 and higher.)

As was true with formatting disks, archiving files can be a simple or complex procedure.

In this lesson you've learned how to archive disk files and use the Backup utility. The next lesson shows you how to perform a total backup of all files on your hard disk.

Lesson 21
Backing Up a
Hard Disk

In this lesson you'll learn how to perform a total backup of all files on your hard disk.

Performing a Total Backup

One of the most common Backup procedures is a total backup, where you archive all files existing on a hard disk, including the files in any subdirectories it contains, to already formatted target disks. Essentially, this procedure creates a "clone" of your entire hard disk structure. A total backup of drive C is the default backup operation. Use the following steps to archive all the files currently on your drive C hard disk:

1. Display the Backup Fixed Disk dialog box, as described in Lesson 20.

2. Type the parameters C:*.* a: 15, as shown in Figure 21.1.

3. Click on OK or press Enter.

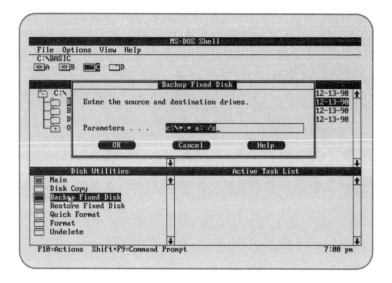

Figure 21-1. Parameters required to back up all files on drive C to drive A.

DOS prompts you to insert your first target disk (backup diskette 01) in drive A. As an added precaution, DOS also warns you that any data currently residing on that disk will be erased during the subsequent backup operation. At this message, use the following steps to begin the actual backup:

1. Insert a blank, formatted or unformatted disk into drive A.

2. Close the drive door.

3. Press any key.

MS-DOS 5 begins the backup operations, listing all of your files as they are copied to the target disk. Usually, the disk space required to archive your files will be larger than a single disk. Exactly how many target disks you'll need depends on what type of disks you are using. For example, backing up 20-megabytes of data requires approximately fourteen 3-1/2", 1.44M disks. When the first target disk is filled, you will be prompted to remove it and insert another disk in drive A. Repeat this sequence as many times as needed to back up all the specified files.

MS-DOS 5 displays the following message when the backup operation is completed:

```
Press any key to return to MS-DOS Shell
```

To end the backup operation, press any key.

Formatting Disks During a Backup

MS-DOS 5 allows you to specify a different disk size and density for a backup format just as you can for a regular format, by adding a *size* parameter, as follows:

C:*.* A: /s /f:*size*

Size options are given in Lesson 7.

Although the total backup is a relatively common operation, it is not the only kind of backup you can perform. The following sections outline several other popular backup procedures.

Backing Up Selected Subdirectories

You may not always want or need to back up an entire hard disk. For example, you may have organized your directory structure to include special subdirectories used to store data files that change often. If this is the case, you would need to back up only the constantly changing files on a regular basis.

127

Including a directory name in the *drive1* path tells MS-DOS 5 to back up only the files in that directory. For example, to selectively back up files currently stored in your DOS subdirectory, you would enter the following parameters at the Backup Fixed Disk dialog box:

C:\DOS*.* A:

In this case, only those files stored in the specified subdirectory, DOS, would be archived.

Backing Up Selected Files

You can refine the preceding process one step further and select only one group of files in a subdirectory to archive. Suppose, for example, that you need to back up only the COM files located in your DOS subdirectory. To accomplish this, enter the following information at the Backup Fixed Disk dialog box:

C:\DOS*.COM A:

Backing Up Modified Files Only

One popular use for the Backup utility is to update your archive disks by copying only those files that you have changed since you performed the last backup operation. During a backup operation, MS-DOS 5 stamps each file with a date and time, identifying when it was last backed up. The **/m** switch enables you to archive only those files that have been modified since the previous backup was performed. For example, enter the following parameters at the Backup Fixed Disk dialog box to back up only those files in the DOS directory that have changed since the previous backup:

C:\DOS*.* A: /m /a

Including the **/a** switch in this command adds the modified files to your BACKUP disks, without overwriting previous versions.

Archived but not Accessible You cannot use files created by the Backup utility for normal PC operations. They are, in the truest sense of the word, for archival purposes only. Before you can incorporate these archive files back into your day-to-day PC activities, you must reconstruct them in standard DOS format using the Restore Fixed Disk utility, which also can be found in the Disk Utilities program group.

The DOS Shell Backup Fixed Disk utility is perhaps the most important utility included with MS-DOS 5. The data files you create in the course of your day-to-day PC operations are the most valuable resource you have. Disk failures happen only rarely, but they do happen. When a disk fails, the files it contains can be destroyed. Backing up your hard disks regularly is the easiest way to prevent such an occurrence from turning into a total disaster.

In this lesson you've learned how to use the DOS Shell Backup Fixed Disk utility to archive your hard disk files. In the next lesson you'll learn how to work with the DOS system prompt.

Working from the DOS System Prompt

In this lesson you'll learn how to exit the DOS Shell and enter commands at the MS-DOS 5 system prompt. You'll also review basic DOS commands used in this book.

The System Prompt Alternative

As helpful as the DOS Shell is, some people prefer to work from outside that environment. Additionally, there are certain activities that should never be initiated from within the DOS Shell. **CHKDSK**, for instance, is one example of a command that you should always enter at the DOS system prompt after unloading the DOS Shell completely from memory. You can either temporarily suspend the DOS Shell, work at the system prompt, and then return to the DOS Shell, or you can completely exit the DOS Shell.

Temporarily Suspending the DOS Shell and Displaying the System Prompt

For relatively straightforward procedures such as changing the date and time recorded in your system clock, the logical choice is to temporarily suspend the DOS Shell but not remove it completely from memory. Use the following key-combination command, displayed on the DOS Shell status line, to temporarily suspend the DOS Shell and access the system prompt:

• Press Shift+F9.

The DOS Shell screen is replaced by the standard DOS system prompt. The Shift+F9 command does not completely unload the DOS Shell from memory. Rather, it suspends DOS Shell and lets you temporarily access the DOS system prompt. When you're finished entering commands at the system prompt, use the following steps to return to the DOS Shell:

1. Type EXIT.

2. Press Enter.

Exiting the DOS Shell and Using Standard DOS Commands

If the activities you expect to perform from the system prompt include making fundamental changes to your PC environment—for example, checking the integrity of your hard disk—then you should close the DOS Shell down completely before proceeding. Use the following steps to unload the DOS Shell completely from memory and access the MS-DOS 5 system prompt:

1. Select **File** from the DOS Shell menu.

2. Select **Exit**.

This completely removes the DOS Shell from memory and displays the MS-DOS 5 system prompt.

Two-key Exit You can press Alt+F4 to bypass the File menu and unload the DOS Shell from memory with a simple two-key command.

DOS Commands

MS-DOS 5 is really a group of procedures, commands, and special programs you use to control and manage your PC environment, much like any other applications program. What makes DOS special is that its programs help other programs run on your computer.

Like virtually all PC operations, a DOS command can be as simple or as complex as the current situation demands. At their simplest, you can perform DOS operations by issuing a single command, as is the case when using the **DIR** command to view a simple listing of files in the current directory. You can also use the **DIR** command to print a listing, sorted by file size, of all PIC (graphic) files in the C:\LOTUS\DATA subdirectory. To support such precise operations, most MS-DOS 5 commands support a variety of special command modifiers, similar to the parameters you've already entered into various dialog boxes when working within the DOS Shell. This lesson also includes exercises designed to familiarize you with executing commands from the MS-DOS 5 system prompt.

Entering DOS Commands

Entering commands at the DOS system prompt is a three-step process:

1. Type in the appropriate DOS command for the procedure you want to perform.

2. Add any parameters needed to specify precisely how this command should be executed.

3. Press Enter to tell MS-DOS 5 to execute this command.

Step two is optional and used only if you want to change the way in which a command normally executes. The following steps, for example, will cause the DIR command to display a list of files in the current directory:

1. Type **DIR**.

2. Press Enter.

After executing this command, your screen will resemble Figure 22-1, which shows a sample directory listing on drive C. This screen contains the following information:

- The volume label for drive C (ZENITH 286).

- A serial number that MS-DOS assigned to drive C during formatting (1631-B037).

- The name of the directory in which these files are stored (C:\).

- A listing of any subdirectories running off this directory, identified by the <DIR> notation, along with the date and time these directories were created.

133

- Individual listings for each file, containing that file's name, its size in bytes, and the date and time it was last modified.

- The total number of files in this directory (9) and their total storage requirements (55,783 bytes).

- The amount of storage space still available on this disk (31,084,544 bytes).

```
C:\>DIR

Volume in drive C is ZENITH 286
Volume Serial Number is 1631-B037
Directory of C:\

DOS              <DIR>        01-17-91    9:46p
OLD_DOS    1     <DIR>        01-17-91    9:46p
COMMAND    COM    46246  12-13-90    4:09a
WINA20     386     9349  12-13-90    4:09a
CONFIG     SYS       60  01-17-91   10:01p
AUTOEXEC   BAT       64  01-17-91   10:01p
BATCH            <DIR>        01-22-91    6:54p
AUTOEXEC   HLD       64  01-17-91   10:01p
BASIC            <DIR>        01-25-91    7:06p
           9 file(s)       55783 bytes
                        31084544 bytes free

C:\>
```

Figure 22-1. A default directory listing.

You can add parameters to the **DIR** command to change its appearance and contents. For example, follow these steps to display a file listing for the DOS directory on drive C:

1. Type **DIR C:\DOS**.

2. Press Enter.

134

To see the names of all the files in a large directory, add the parameter **/W**. For example,

1. Type **DIR C:\DOS /W**.

2. Press Enter.

Your screen should resemble Figure 22-2, which shows the DOS directory listing formatted to a wide display. This listing omits additional information such as file size, date, and time.

```
Volume in drive C is ZENITH 286
Volume Serial Number is 1631-B037
Directory of C:\DOS

[.]             [..]            EGA.SYS         DISPLAY.SYS     FORMAT.COM
PACKING.LST     ANSI.SYS        COUNTRY.SYS     HIMEM.SYS       KEYB.COM
KEYBOARD.SYS    MODE.COM        SETVER.EXE      SYS.COM         UNFORMAT.COM
DEBUG.EXE       DOSKEY.COM      EDLIN.EXE       EMM386.EXE      FASTOPEN.EXE
FC.EXE          FDISK.EXE       MEM.EXE         MIRROR.COM      MORE.COM
RAMDRIVE.SYS    SHARE.EXE       SMARTDRV.SYS    UNDELETE.EXE    XCOPY.EXE
DOSSHELL.VID    DOSSHELL.INI    DOSSHELL.COM    DOSSHELL.EXE    DOSSHELL.GRB
DOSSWAP.EXE     EXE2BIN.EXE     PRINT.EXE       REPLACE.EXE     TREE.COM
DOSSHELL.HLP    EDIT.HLP        RECOVER.EXE     DOSHELP.HLP     HELP.EXE
QBASIC.HLP      EDIT.COM        MSHERC.COM      QBASIC.EXE      APPEND.EXE
ATTRIB.EXE      BACKUP.EXE      CHKDSK.EXE      COMP.EXE        DISKCOMP.COM
DISKCOPY.COM    FIND.EXE        LABEL.EXE       RESTORE.EXE     SORT.EXE
4201.CPI        4208.CPI        5202.CPI        ASSIGN.COM      DRIVER.SYS
EGA.CPI         EXPAND.EXE      README.TXT      NETWORKS.TXT    UMB.TXT
GRAFTABL.COM    GRAPHICS.COM    GRAPHICS.PRO    JOIN.EXE        LCD.CPI
NLSFUNC.EXE     PRINTER.SYS     SUBST.EXE       CLEANUP.EXE     CLEANUP.INF
COMMAND.COM     MOUSE.COM       808DDOSC.BAT
        83 file(s)    2035182 bytes
                     31084544 bytes free

C:\>
```

Figure 22-2. Using parameters to give you greater control over how a DOS command is executed.

MS-DOS Command Summary

This section briefly describes basic DOS commands referenced in this book. Each command is followed by a brief description of what that command does and the proper

135

syntax for entering that command at the DOS system prompt. This command summary is provided as a quick reference only. For more information on the DOS commands, you should refer to your MS-DOS documentation.

CD (CHDIR)
Used to display or change the currently active directory.

> CD [*drive*:][*path*]

CHKDSK
Used to display information about a specific disk or directory—how many files it contains, how many bytes of storage space are unused, whether any lost clusters exist, and so on—or, alternatively, an individual file.

> CHKDSK [*drive*:][*path*][*filename*] [*/f*] [*/v*]

Where:

> [*drive*:][*path*] identifies the drive, directory, or files you want to check.
> */f* tells DOS to convert any lost clusters it discovers into temporary files.
> */v* displays the name of each file as it is checked.

CLS
Clears the screen and redisplays the DOS system prompt.

COPY
Used to copy one or more files to another disk or directory or, alternatively, to make a duplicate copy of a file with a different name in that file's original directory.

> COPY [*source file(s)*] [*destination file(s)*] [*/v*]

Where:

> [*source file(s)*] indicates those files you want to copy, including its path notation. You can use DOS wild-card characters to copy multiple files.
>
> [*destination file(s)*] indicates where the files should be copied to. You can use DOS wild-card characters to indicate multiple destinations.
>
> */v* tells DOS to verify that all files were written correctly to the destination disk.

DATE
Used to display or change the current system date.

DEL (ERASE)
Used to erase a specified file or group of files.

> **DEL** [*drive*:][*path*][*filename*] [*/p*]

Where:

> [*drive*:][*path*] identifies the drive, directory, or files you want to delete.
>
> */p* tells DOS to prompt you to verify a file deletion before actually erasing it from the disk.

DIR
Displays a listing of the files stored in a specified directory, as described in previous sections of this lesson.

DISKCOPY
Used to create an exact duplicate of a floppy disk on a second disk of the same type.

> **DISKCOPY** [*drive1*] [*drive2*] [*/1*] [*/v*]

Where:

> [*drive1*] indicates the source disk.
> [*drive2*] indicates the destination disk.
> */1* specifies that only the first side of a double-sided disk should be duplicated.
> */v* tells DOS to verify that the disk was duplicated correctly.

DOSSHELL
Used to start the DOS Shell.

EXIT
Used to exit the DOS system prompt and return to a temporarily suspended DOS Shell session.

FORMAT
Prepares a disk for data storage, as described in Lessons 6 and 7.

> **FORMAT** [*drive:*] [*/v:label*] [*/f:size*] [*/s*] [*/t:tracks*] [*/n:sectors*] [*/1*] [*/4*] [*/8*]

Format is described in detail in Lessons 6 and 7.

MD (MKDIR)
Used to create a new directory or subdirectory on a disk.

> MD [*drive:*] *path*

Where:

> [*drive:*] specifies the drive on which you want the new directory created.
> *path* is the path name for the new directory.

PATH
Used to display or specify a command search path.

PATH [*drive:path*];[*drive:path*];...[*drive:path*]

Where:

[*drive:path*] is a list of any directories you want included in the command search path; you must separate multiple directories with a semicolon (;).

REN (RENAME)
Used to change the name of a specified file or group of files.

REN [*drive:path*]*oldfilename(s) newfilename(s)*

Where:

[*drive:path*]*oldfilename(s)* specifies the location and name of the file you want to rename. You can use DOS wild-card characters to rename multiple files with a single **REN** command.
newfilename(s) specifies the new name for these files.

TYPE
Used to display the contents of a text (ASCII) file to your system monitor.

TYPE [*drive*:][*path*] *filename*

Where:

[*drive*:][*path*]*filename* identifies the location and name of the file whose contents you want displayed.

139

UNDELETE
Used to recover files accidentally erased with a DEL command.

UNDELETE [*drive*:][*path*] *filename* [*/list*] [*/all*]

Where:

[*drive*:][*path*] *filename(s)* identifies the location and name of the files you want to undelete.
/list displays a list of deleted files that are recoverable.
/all automatically recovers all deleted files without prompting you for confirmation.

VER
Displays the version (release) of DOS currently running on your system.

VOL
Used to display the volume label and serial number of a disk.

VOL [*drive*:]

Where:

[*drive*:] indicates the disk for which you want label and serial number information.

Summary

In this lesson you've learned the fundamentals of entering a command at the MS-DOS 5 system prompt. As you've seen throughout this book, corresponding MS-DOS 5 commands exist for virtually all DOS Shell procedures. Once you're comfortable using the DOS Shell, your own curiosity will probably motivate you to learn more about entering and executing commands from the MS-DOS system prompt.

Index

Symbols

* (asterisk) wild-card
   character, 71-74
/F: parameters, 39
? (question mark) wild-card
   character, 71-74
[ ] (brackets), 10

―――――― A ――――――

accessing file listings, 68
Add Group dialog box, 105-106
Add Program dialog box, 108
Advanced Properties dialog
   box, 110
Alt+F4 (Exit) key
   combination, 16
analyzing disks, 41-43
application programs, 63
ASCII text files, 139
asterisk (*) wild-card
   character, 71-74
AUTOEXEC.BAT file, 98-100
   editing, 102

―――――― B ――――――

backing up
   files, 125-127

hard disks, 125-127
modified files, 128-129
selected files, 128
subdirectories, 127
Backup Fixed Disk Utility,
   121-124
Backup Utility options, 123-124
BASIC directory, 58
BASIC subdirectory, 54-56
BATCH directory, 49
booting
   cold, 1-2
   warm, 1-2
brackets ([ ]), 10
built-in safeguards, 59-60

―――――― C ――――――

canceling
   DOS Shell operation, 11
   multiple file selection, 47
CD (CHDIR) command, 136
changing
   areas in DOS Shell, 10-11
   directories, 136
   graphics displays, 18-20

CHKDSK command, 43, 136
clicking, 16-17
cold booting, 1-2
commands
  CD (CHDIR), 136
  CHKDSK, 43, 136
  COPY, 136
  DATE, 137
  DEL, 84
  DEL (ERASE), 137
  Delete, 59
  DIR, 133-134, 137
  DISKCOPY, 137
  DOSSHELL, 138
  EXIT, 138
  FORMAT, 138
  format parameters, 38-39
  MD (MKDIR), 138
  PATH, 139
  RD (Remove Directory), 61
  REN (RENAME), 139
  TYPE, 139
  UNDELETE, 97, 140
  VER, 140
  VOL, 140
context-sensitive help, 22-23
controlling disks, 10
COPY command, 136
copying
  files, 75-78, 84, 137
  system files to disk, 35-37
Ctrl+Alt+Del (warm reboot) key
  combination, 1

——————— D ———————

data files, 24, 62-63
DATE command, 137
date prompts, 3
DEL (ERASE) command, 137
DEL command, 84
Delete command, 59

Delete Directory Confirmation
  dialog box, 58
Delete File Confirmation dialog
  box, 93
deleting files, 92-96
device drivers, 16
dialog boxes, 20
  Add Group, 105-106
  Add Program, 108
  Advanced Properties, 110
  Delete Directory
    Confirmation, 58
  Delete File Confirmation, 93
  Format, 30
  New Program Object, 106
  Rename File, 79
  Run, 116
  Screen Display Mode, 19
  Search File, 86
DIR command, 133-134, 137
directories
  BATCH, 49, 51
  changing, 136
  creating, 49-51
  displaying, 137
  organizing files, 27-28
  removing, 57-61
Directory Tree, 4
  collapsing, 53
  expanding, 51-52
disk capacity, 27
Disk Utilities option, 10
Disk Utilities program
  group, 29
DISKCOPY command, 137
disks, 24
  analyzing, 41-43
  formatting, 29-31, 39, 138
  while backing up, 127

disks/drives, 26
  assigning volume labels,
    31-33
  controlling disks, 10
  floppy, 25-26
  hard, 25-26
  selecting active drives, 9
  specifying formats, 37
  volume labels, 140
displaying
  directories, 137
  pull-down menus, 14
DOS
  commands, 131-134
  Command Summary, 135
  exiting, 138
  files, 64
DOS Shell, 130-131
  canceling operation, 11
  changing areas, 10-11
  exiting, 131-32
  exiting with speed keys, 16
  Family Tree, 53-56
  file listing, 65
  keyboard commands, 7-8
  pull-down menus, 14
  quitting, 5-6
  returning to, 43
  running from keyboard, 7
  screen, 5
  Search option, 85-91
  starting, 4, 138
  View File Contents
    option, 98-100
DOSSHELL command, 138
double-clicking, 16-17
dragging, 16-17
drive listing, 4

—— E ——

editing
  AUTOEXEC.BAT file, 102
entering DOS commands,
  133-134
EXIT command, 138
exiting
  DOS, 138
  DOS Shell, 131-132
  MS-DOS Editor, 103

—— F ——

F10 (Actions) function key, 5
file listing, 65
file listings, 4, 65-66
  accessing, 68
  rearranging, 69-70
  sorting, 70-71
files, 24, 62
  ASCII text, 139
  AUTOEXEC.BAC, 98-100
  backing up, 121, 125-129
  copying, 75-78, 84, 137
  data, 24, 62-63
  deleting, 92-96
  DOS, 64
  extensions, 72-74
  graphics icon, 66-67
  listing, 65-66
  marking, 71
  moving, 81-84
  multiple, 44-46
  organizing with
    directories, 27-28
  program, 24, 62-63
  protecting, 121-123
  recovering after deletion,
    94-96

relocating, 81-84
renaming, 78-80
saving after editing, 103
searching, 85-91
selecting for searches, 88
system, 35-37
viewing, 98-100
floppy disks/drives, 25-26
loading MS-DOS, 2-3
FORMAT command, 138
format command
parameters, 38-39
Format dialog box, 30
formatting
disks, 29-39, 138
while backing up, 127
system disks, 35-37
function keys, 15-16

──────── G-L ────────

graphics changing displays,
18-20
hard disks/drives, 25-26
backing up, 125-127
loading MS-DOS, 2-3
help, 20-23
key combinations
Alt+F4 (Exit), 16
Ctrl+Alt+Del (warm
reboot), 1
Keyboard Help topic list, 21
loading
from floppy disk/drive, 2-3
from hard disk/drive, 2-3

──────── M ────────

Main program group
listings, 11

marking
files, 71
multiple files, 44-46
MD (MKDIR) command, 138
menu bar, 4
menus pull-down, 8, 14
modifying group program
items, 109-112
mouse, 16
clicking, 16-17
double-clicking, 16-17
dragging, 16-17
pointing, 16-17
moving
files, 81-84
to program group
window, 10-11
MS-DOS 5
Editor, 100-101
MS-DOS Editor, 103
multiple files
canceling selection, 47
displaying information, 44
marking, 44-46
storing, 46
multiple format parameters, 40
multiple programs, 113-116

──────── N-P ────────

New Program Object dialog
box, 106
Options menu
Show Information option,
41-43
parameters
/F:, 39
adding to DIR command, 134
multiple format, 40
PATH command, 139

PATH statement, 100
pointing, 16-17
program files, 24, 62-63
program group window, 4
    moving to, 10-11
program groups, 29, 105-108
    adding items, 107-108
    choosing items, 109
    creating, 104-106
    modifying items, 109-112
programs
    adding to task list, 117-118
    removing from task list,
        118-120
prompts, 3
    date, 3
    system, 3, 130-131
    time, 3
protecting files, 122-123
pull-down menus, 8
    displaying, 14

——— Q-R ———

question mark (?) wild-card
    character, 71-74
quitting
    DOS Shell, 5-6
RD (Remove Directory)
    command, 61
recovering deleted files, 94-96
relocating files, 81-84
removing
    BASIC directory, 58
    directories, 57-61
    programs from task
        lists, 118-120
REN (RENAME)
    command, 139
Rename File dialog box, 79

renaming files, 78-80
returning to DOS Shell, 43
root directory file listing, 65
Run dialog box, 116

——— S ———

saving edited files, 103
Screen Display Mode dialog
    box, 19
screens, 5
scrolling, 12-13
Search File dialog box, 86
searching files, 85-91
sorting file listings, 70-71
specifying disk formats, 37
speed keys, *see* function keys
starting
    Backup Fixed Disk
        Utility, 121
    DOS Shell, 4, 138
    MS-DOS 5 Editor, 100-101
storing multiple files, 46
subdirectories
    backing up, 127
    creating, 54-56
system disks formatting, 35-37
system files, 35-37
system prompts, 3, 130-131

——— T ———

task lists
    adding programs, 115-118
    removing programs, 118-120
task swapping, 113-116, 120
time prompts, 3
TYPE command, 139

U-Z

UNDELETE command,
    97, 140
VER command, 140
viewing
    file listings, 65
    files, 98-100
VOL command, 140
volume labels, 31-33, 140
warm booting, 1-2
wild-card characters, 71-74
    * (asterisk), 71-74
    ? (question mark), 71-74